MORE THAN A DIAGNOSIS

Connect with Us: The stories in this compilation and others like them—along with resources, articles, and other tools for parents—can be found at **thebrainpossible.com.** To connect specifically with the stories included in this book, visit **thebrainpossible.com/more-than-a-diagnosis.**

A Note to Our Community: In this book, you will not find the term "special needs" outside of direct quotes. That's because at The Brain Possible, our goal is to change the conversation around childhood brain injury from one of limitations to one of hope and possibility. We prefer to use "differently-abled," as it feels more empowering and authentic to our mission. Anytime we can drop a label, we go for it.

That said, we know many parents and caregivers embrace the term "special needs," and we certainly respect that decision.

We believe all children are beautiful and— yes—special. And differently-abled. Both are true, and we are all in this together.

Disclaimer: The Brain Possible *does not* provide medical advice, diagnosis, or treatment recommendations. It *does* provide resources, information, and hope.

more than a diagnosis

Stories of hurdles, hope, and possibility from parents of children who are differently-abled

Jessica Burdg *for THE BRAIN POSSIBLE*

LIONCREST
PUBLISHING

MORE THAN A DIAGNOSIS
Stories of Hurdles, Hope, and Possibility from
Parents of Children Who Are Differently-Abled

ISBN   978-1-5445-1508-3 *Hardcover*
       978-1-5445-1509-0 *Paperback*
       978-1-5445-1507-6 *Ebook*

To all the parents and children I have met along this journey, and to all I have yet to meet as I continue this project in the future. Your stories have both broken my heart into pieces and filled it with awe and joy. Thank you for who you are and how you move through the world—and most of all, thank you for letting me glimpse a small part of your overwhelming will and overwhelming love. You have and will continue to change me.

To every mother, father, stepparent, grandparent, sibling—any family, chosen or biological—of a child who is differently-abled. Or any child, for that matter. This "'raising kids'" thing is hard, and it is filled with such beauty. I didn't use "but" for a reason because the two are not mutually exclusive. Know that I see you, and this book is for you, too.

To every child, no matter your circumstance. I think you are wonderful just as you are, and I am so thankful you're here.

Finally, to my daughters, Ella and Emmylou. You're little now, but what I always tell you is true even (and especially) as you grow: anytime you don't know what to do, simply pick the kind thing. Every. Single. Time. Keep being inclusive and doing what's right as you branch out there in the big, wild world. I know you will. I love you.

CONTENTS

FOREWORD

By Emily Abbott
April 22, 2020

WHEN MY HUSBAND MATT AND I LOST OUR SON Carter at only twenty months old to complications from a brain injury he sustained as a newborn, we vowed to carry on his spirit of hope and joy. One piece of that has been forming The Brain Possible, a foundation that provides resources, information, and hope to families like yours.

I learned a lot during and after my too-short but beautiful journey with my son. One of the most important cornerstones, for me, was to find people who have walked this road before. I know firsthand that having a child with a complex condition means that you—parents and caregivers—may need to step into a new version of yourselves. You have more of an opportunity to become researchers, advocates, therapists, cheerleaders, influencers, citizen scientists, and warriors. This is a job that can push you to your limits. It may cause many sleepless nights, adrenal fatigue, and sometimes even isolation.

My point? We need each other.

The one thing that helped me find direction, answers, and the strength to step into my new role—which I readily admit was not easy, as I did (and sometimes still do) have moments of shock and grief—was hearing from other families. First, there was seeing the beauty in other people's circumstances like mine. Then came the hope that I could do this because other people before me have done it and continue to do it every day. I learned that there is no reason we have to be alone and think about every challenge coming at us as if we are the first ones faced with them, putting in the extra work to build therapeutic and home/life solutions from scratch. We do not always need to reinvent the wheel when we can find out what has (and hasn't) worked for others.

That is where the magic is: in finding connection and support from other families who have walked even a mile ahead of you. By sharing the stories you are about to read, these families are helping so many who are seeking, grieving, feeling lost, and facing complex diagnoses.

In my listening of other people's stories, I also woke up to how we are all connected in this life. I learned how common so many neurological conditions are. I learned that bad things do happen to good people, every single day. I learned that there is so much that I don't know and I should know, and I became thirsty for information and for ways to do and be better.

I became drawn to families who chose to look beyond their child's diagnosis. In fact, I began to seek out those families pushing the limitations and carving out full, beautiful lives for themselves and their families. Families who didn't focus on what they were told their child would never do, but instead wondered what they *could do*. Families who put blinders on to the noise of gloom and doom, of negative predictions or assumptions. Those were my people. Those still are my people. I was forever changed, I ascended into a new and evolved version of myself. Empowered. Strong. Resilient. Informed. Knowledgeable. Ready to share all of that with you.

I believe in miracles because I have seen them in others. I don't pay attention to what the odds are. Miracles, by definition, defy reason, and I'm proud to live my life unreasonably. I have no room for limitations or labels, and I'm inspired by others who embody this belief as well. There is beauty in our children. There is beauty in our circumstances. Read these stories, hear from our community, and be changed.

INTRODUCTION

DURING ONE OF THE INTERVIEWS FOR THIS BOOK, I was a bit late because I had a meeting at my oldest daughter's school to discuss her Individualized Education Program (IEP)—a simple one for a stutter, nothing else. Certainly nothing major.

When I finally got on the phone, I quickly apologized for my tardiness, gave my reasoning, and tried to jump into the interview to make up time. But the mother on the other end of the line would not let me. Instead, she asked about my daughter. She said a stutter sounded hard for a little girl coming into her own socially. She asked questions. All this when we were about to dive into *her* experience with her daughter's significant brain injury, the gravity of the issue on a different level, by all rights.

I had a meeting about my daughter's stutter while her daughter may never speak, and she wanted to talk about how *I* felt? She wanted to hold space for *me* and listen? I was flabbergasted. This wasn't apples to oranges. These orchards were on different planets. When I brought that up, she dismissed my pushback, saying, "It all counts."

This example embodies a grace and an unyielding acceptance that I have experienced over and over again when speaking with the many families for the More than a Diagnosis project—one we initially titled Stories of Hope. Over the course of a year and change (so far), I interviewed mothers and fathers who astounded me with both their strength and their softness. With their willingness to share their stories with me—a stranger to them, in those early meetings—knowing at the time only that doing so may help someone else navigate a challenging diagnosis. That's it. Their children have cerebral palsy, autism, cystic fibrosis, dyslexia, spina bifida, Down syndrome, epilepsy, rare genetic conditions, traumatic brain injuries, or severe complications from brain-damaging viruses—I could go on.

And yet.

They took the time, that precious time, to share with me. They told me about their lowest lows, about seeing devastating test results, about how it hurt when people averted their eyes on the street, about their worries for the future. And we cried. They also told me about miraculous advancements their children had made, about their pride, about what gifts their children are. And we cried some more.

There is no tangible reward in that, in baring your sorrow and your truth and your beauty. But they did it. I was warmed during each conversation—even moreso because, throughout this project, the common refrain has been one of gratitude for simple moments. For not what these parents have been able to teach their children, but the other way around.

THIS BOOK IS NOT MINE

I am an advocate for the differently-abled community and editorial chair at The Brain Possible, a nonprofit that provides resources and hope for families of children faced with challenging diagnoses. I am also a writer with a passion for personal narratives and a person with a passion for helping people share stories that matter. It was logical to combine these, so the seeds of the More than a Diagnosis project were sown. What was (and still is) an ongoing blog series profiling children who are differently-abled and their families has bloomed into this book. Who knows? Maybe one day we'll have a whole garden.

While it is true that I have written each of the stories in this book, this is decidedly *not* my story. I composed these profiles directly from personal interviews I conducted with each of the families included here, and they have graciously allowed me to share them with the world. This is their book, not mine. It belongs to these families and the entire differently-abled community. The bottom line? This is a collection of stories that deserve to be told, and I am so grateful for having the chance to have heard them firsthand.

That's a big reason why **100 percent of the proceeds**

from the sale of this book will go to Who Is Carter, the parent and funding foundation for The Brain Possible.

It has been my honor to learn from these families and help them share their authentic journeys, both the dim parts and those filled with such light. My hope is that the funding from the sale of this book will help us reach more families and ensure I am able to continue More than a Diagnosis for as long as there are hopeful stories to be told. Which, if you ask me, will be forever.

FORWARD TOGETHER

At the end of the day, just as that mother reminded me when she asked about my daughter on the phone all those months ago, so much softens when we see others not as in comparison to us *but as simply people*. When we treat them that way. When we actively reject that anything has to be a competition, we can see every mother and father, every baby and teen, for who they are regardless of diagnoses or labels: worthy of our love and kindness and care, and nothing less. No matter what.

In Ben Lerner's novel *The Topeka School*, we meet a character who often quasi-quotes Danish physicist, Niels Bohr, specifically, his theory that states:

> "The opposite of a truth is a falsehood; but the opposite of a profound truth...may be another profound truth...if I assert it's August when it isn't—simply false; but if I say that life is

pain, that is true, profoundly so; so, too, that life is joy; the more profound the statement, the more reversible..."

It's that last sentence in this passage that has stuck with me—the piece about reversibility. I have never claimed to "know what it's like" for the families I speak with for this project on a daily basis. I do not know for certain the reversible profound truths families with children who are differently-abled hold. That said, from our conversations, I might be able to loosely ballpark those profound truths somewhere in the neighborhoods that house two big ones: fear and hope.

I don't have to understand what it's like at the intersection of the two to recognize that it exists. That it's sometimes beautiful and sometimes hard and at all times human. To hold space for it. To ask questions. To admit that I will *never* "get it" and—rather than turn my back or avert my eyes—to listen all the harder for it.

Listening hard for this project has and continues to be one of my most heartbreaking and heartbuilding endeavors. Nothing has ever been more worth it. I firmly believe we are all better if we move forward together, and this is my way of doing that.

In the spirit of moving forward together, if you'd like to connect specifically with the stories and families included in this book, please join us at thebrainpossible. com/more-than-a-diagnosis. We'll be waiting for you.

However you have found your way to this book, I hope

you leave it with this, as Anna Enos (Sammy's mother whom you'll meet later in the book) told me once on the phone, "Hope is a religion in this house." So, I would say, is opening your heart and listening. Because when one child or one family wins, we all do.

It all counts.

GABE'S STORY

GABE, KNOCKING ON ELEVEN'S DOOR, IS SWEET, AFFEC-tionate, and kind. He is a joy to be around and an expert at connecting well with people—whether that's his mother Nicole, her partner Caroline, or a person he's never met. One of his favorite activities in the world is listening to music, so much so that some type of music or another plays all day in his home. He often hums along, communicating his emotions through music and sound.

Though his affection for those he loves and his affinity for music are common human experiences, there is something about Gabe that is a little less common: he is autistic, and he has Attention Deficit Hyperactivity Disorder (ADHD).

Today, Gabe understands everything but has difficulty following multistep instructions. He doesn't have awareness of dangers and needs help with most everything. He is nonverbal and uses a communication device to interact. He is in an Applied Behavior Analysis (ABA)-based 2:1 class at school, where he learns, socializes, and furthers his motor planning.

While Nicole acknowledges the challenges of raising a son with autism and ADHD, she is also quick to acknowledge the overwhelming joy Gabe brings to her family. They choose to fill their days, while sometimes more difficult than others, with fun, love, and positivity.

"Even though Gabe is nonverbal, his receptive language is strong," Nicole says. "He's incredibly intelligent because he's able to figure out a way to get his needs met nonverbally. That's amazing."

A lot about Gabe is, in fact, amazing. As is a lot about Nicole, who lost her husband Seth while she was pregnant with Gabe, her only child. She weathered many storms alone as a new mother and widow, her family living states away.

Those early years, Nicole recalls, were tough, but she gave her all. Gabe was involved in early intervention occupational and speech therapies as soon as he was eligible, and he was formally diagnosed with autism at a year and a half—a little earlier than the typical two-year diagnosis, yet the doctors were confident.

"We knew at just over a year," Nicole says. "He wasn't talking, pointing, or responding. If I said his name, he'd stare at the fan. He'd turn his trucks upside down and just spin the wheels."

Gabe continued each of his therapies three times weekly—adding daily ABA post-diagnosis—through the county at first, then privately.

"I wanted to give him the best shot," Nicole says. "They say early intervention is the most important. They say up until five years, do all you can. So, I did. I don't know where we'd be today if I hadn't done every possible thing."

Doing every possible thing wasn't easy. Nicole often ran on no sleep—literally—because Gabe himself barely slept. But she went all-in, relying on babysitters she trusted to give her a break now and then and going to therapy to process her grief.

"I didn't know anybody," Nicole recalls of that time. "I didn't have the same friends I'd had before because we no longer had anything in common. I didn't know anyone who had kids with autism."

Since then, a lot has changed. Once Nicole found a group of parents whose children faced needs similar to Gabe's, she reached out and found community. About three years ago, Gabe's medical team found the right dosages of medications to assist both his difficulty with sleeping and his severe ADHD. That, coupled with his special bed he cannot get out of, have improved both of their lives for the better.

"We started trying the med thing early on. When he was four, he was on this sleeping medication that worked briefly—until it didn't anymore," Nicole recalls. "Three years ago, we finally got the right concoction of everything. It was a tough road to get there, but when it finally worked, it worked really well."

Gabe is now able to sit and pay attention. He can learn, something that had been challenging before, and is gentle. He is able to communicate his needs—something Nicole is grateful for.

"There was a period of time when Gabe would come home every day and cry, and I didn't know why," Nicole says. "It turned out to be a gluten allergy. Now, he's on a gluten-free diet and is doing better. It's hard when you don't know what's wrong with your child and they can't tell you. Having the communication device for Gabe has been incredibly helpful."

For parents seeking information or guidance when navigating an autism diagnosis, Nicole has one key hard-won piece of advice: if your child is going to enter a school (and it's not cost-prohibitive), hire an advocate.

Personally, Nicole recalls getting upset—sometimes screaming and crying—during IEP or other service-oriented meetings. She found the low bar of what was offered, the high number of hoops to jump through, and the thick ribbons of red tape to cut overwhelming.

"The teachers really care about him [Gabe], I know they do," Nicole recalls. "But in those meetings, it wasn't about the teachers or what they wanted. Or what we wanted. It was about what the state or county would offer and what we had to do to get it. The services were never enough, and the stipulations were too much. It was all just too much."

Nicole and Gabe's advocate handles the IEP and service discussions now, pushing on Gabe's behalf to ensure he receives the care and services he needs and deserves, and Nicole can focus on her son, not her bureaucratic overwhelm.

That's not to say there aren't worries, of course. Nicole says she thinks often about the long term, which holds many unknowns—especially now, considering she was recently diagnosed with cancer.

"I know Gabe is never going to live independently," Nicole says. "And I want to make life the best it can be for him. I don't trust anyone else to take care of him or trust that arrangement would work for him in the first place, and I know a lot of parents will understand that. So I ask myself: What's important to Gabe? He loves being outside... the beach...the mountains. I'm trying to make that happen. I want him to be happy and safe and taken care of. That's all that matters to me. And that's all any of us can really ask for in life, isn't it? I feel like especially now, we're living in the moment—because all we have is right now."

COOPER'S STORY

COOPER'S MOTHER, ADRIENNE, SAYS SHE NOTICED
things were a little different with Cooper from a young age.
He struggled with fine and gross motor skills, and he had
constant ear infections. When he grew a little older, around
the second grade, she noticed he didn't run the same way

his peers did and that it was more challenging for him to complete basic tasks, like tying his shoes.

During these early years, Adrienne was facing her own struggle: alcohol addiction. She concedes that, with her drinking, there were some symptoms that likely went unnoticed and some opportunities for intervention that went missed. When she joined Alcoholics Anonymous (AA) around the time Cooper was in fifth grade, she recalls reflecting on how much her son had already muscled through in his young life.

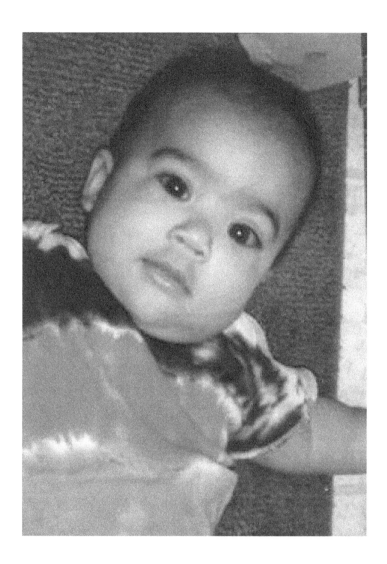

That year, in the thick of her recovery and entry into sobriety, is when it hit Adrienne that there could be something *truly* wrong. She realized Cooper wasn't simply behind and that there was something else at play. What, though? Then, they hit a wall. Cooper began struggling even more.

"He'd fall and scratch his leg, and he'd scream so loudly that you'd have thought he broke his arm," she recalls.

The family explored multiple potential causes, including ADHD, frontal lobe processing delays, and executive function issues. They visited specialist after specialist and tried medication after medication. Cooper spent much of that school year in the principal's office and on so much medication that it was hard for him to stay awake in class. Later that year, Cooper was admitted to a children's psychiatric hospital.

"He'd scream and rock, and we'd have to hold onto him so he didn't hurt himself. He was only in fifth grade," Adrienne recalls. "For me, as a parent and in recovery, that was the hardest thing I've ever had to deal with."

After that stay and with the medications rounding out, Cooper persevered. He did the best he could in school and was, as Adrienne says, "just a really good kid." She eventually talked Cooper into going to Alateen, a group for kids whose parents are recovering alcoholics and addicts. He was reluctant at first, as social situations had long made him uncomfortable.

"When he came out of that first meeting, though, he was smiling ear to ear," Adrienne recalls. "The biggest thing was finding that human connection with people who understood what he'd been through."

Although he felt less alone socially, Cooper still faced challenges in school.

"It was like—you're being told something in class, and

you don't hear everything, only bits and pieces," he says. "A lot of times, they thought I wasn't listening, but I was trying. I thought I was stupid because I couldn't comprehend anything."

Then, at one of her AA meetings, Adrienne was describing what was going on with Cooper—a mixture of ADHD, executive function issues, equilibrium challenges, depression, learning problems in school—a combination of symptoms that Adrienne says makes the journey to diagnosis like "chasing a ghost." A friend referred them to Responsive Centers Psychiatric Care for evaluation and testing.

After testing, the center referred Cooper to one of the most prominent doctors in the field, Dr. Jack Katz. Still, they were told, there was no guarantee he'd be treated in the program, as Cooper's diagnosis was still pending.

Ultimately, Dr. Katz reviewed Cooper's forms and found significant signs of Auditory Processing Disorder (APD), which led to a formal evaluation. Cooper's results clearly showed the presence of APD. Adrienne still remembers the call that he would be seen for therapy.

"I was so relieved, like the world had been lifted off my shoulders," she recounts, sighing. She'd been "banging her head against a wall, praying" for years, she says, to find a name for what Cooper was struggling with—and, more importantly, a solution.

"I was so grateful that this was something a professional could work with him on and NOT ME. Do you know how difficult it is to teach someone all the skills that fall under executive functioning when I struggle with most of those myself?" she says.

The Auditory Processing Therapy program with Dr. Katz has been, according to both Cooper and Adrienne, life changing.

"It's like physical therapy for your ears," Cooper says of the treatment, which (for him) involved repeating words in sequence and at different volumes, listening to sounds over varying background noises Dr. Katz played, and many other techniques. At first, Cooper says the therapy was extremely challenging—sometimes, he couldn't hear the words Dr. Katz wanted him to repeat *at all*. However, after weekly visits—and then biweekly visits, when they started to see improvement—Cooper found success. At fourteen, he can now hear normally.

Cooper and Dr. Katz grew close through therapy, too,

and bonded talking about life, not just about auditory issues. Everyone—Cooper, Adrienne, and Dr. Katz—cried on the last day of therapy.

As for Cooper, he says his life has vastly improved now that he can hear and function more like his peers.

"I have always had an issue with going to talk to other people. A lot of things have been hard for me, like socializing and especially school. I didn't feel like doing it [the work] because I knew the result I was going to get. I hated school because I didn't understand any of it," he says. "Now, I have an 87 in math and I've done all my assignments on my own. It feels much easier to listen, and I understand what the teacher is trying to say. It [Auditory Processing Therapy] changed my life in a very positive way. Not only was it just that, but I got to work with Dr. Katz, and he's the nicest person I've ever met."

Cooper says he hopes other people can learn about Auditory Processing Disorder and the therapy that treats it so they, too, can live fuller lives.

"To all the other people who have this and are out of hope, I just want to tell you that there is something that can help a lot," Cooper says. "I have a lot more going for me now. My world has gotten bigger. Just keep going and trying, and it will work out."

For Adrienne, her prevailing emotion today is gratitude. A mother of four—including a younger son, Parker, who has behavioral issues and severe ADHD—she cultivates an environment of honest communication in her household to help her family stay in that good place, even though it's scary at times. Cooper comes to her openly when he's struggling in school or with medication, for example, and she encourages Parker to do the same.

"It's hard to be in this place. I know nothing about ADHD," she says. "But I knew nothing about Auditory Processing Disorder, either. And here we are. We are still here."

Retrospectively, Adrienne encourages parents to ask questions of physicians and specialists about alternate forms of treatment if the standard options are not fruitful. She says to be persistent and remember that you are advocating for someone who can't advocate for themselves. Also, gain an understanding from your child's perspective and talk to them about what is going on, while being honest and open to hearing what they have to say. Honor their feelings.

She also encourages everyone to take opportunities to help other people whenever possible—like the woman at AA who told her about the testing facility in the first place, and Cooper who was willing to share his story at the young age of fourteen.

Of their journey, Adrienne says, "We've both been broken around the same time, and now we're healing and growing together. It's been an honor to be on this journey with Cooper. I told him just the other day, 'I see you becoming a better human being. I see you taking your adversity and sharing it with other people. I don't know a lot of adults who would do that. This is what makes you a good man.' That's what I'm proud of."

PIPER'S STORY

ASHLEY WOOD AND HER HUSBAND TIM WERE OVER-joyed to discover they were pregnant with twins, after another successful round of IVF (their son, Owen, was another success story, born two and a half years prior). After a bumpy start, Ashley's pregnancy and delivery went smoothly. Piper and Mimi were born vaginally with no complications. All early testing for the girls was clear.

Then, at four months old, Piper had her first seizure. It was a simple partial seizure, where her right arm started to rigidly pulse and pump.

At six months old, Piper had what would be her first grand mal seizure, one that would forever alter the lives of her entire family. Ashley recalls this day vividly. They were on Harbour Island, one of the Bahamian islands, spending a week with Ashley's mother and sisters as a gathering since her father passed away from melanoma in the fall of 2006. It was December 31, 2009, the last night of the trip, around 5:00 pm. Tim had Mimi in his lap, and Ashley had

Piper. They were about to go to dinner, but Ashley needed to change Piper's diaper first. On the changing table, Piper launched into a full-on grand mal seizure that lasted for over an hour.

Ashley grabbed her and started running down the boardwalk screaming for help. She remembers a man running toward her saying he was a neurologist. He confirmed Piper was having a seizure. One of the employees at the hotel offered his truck, and Ashley, Tim, Piper, and Ashley's sister hopped in the front seat. They raced off to meet a doctor at the island's only medical site—a clinic set up in a cinderblock building.

The drive was rough and bumpy on the island's dirt roads. It seemed to be taking forever to get to the doctor. "She was turning blue and foaming at the mouth," Ashley recalls. "I thought she was dying."

But she wasn't.

Once the seizing stopped, the doctor wanted Piper airlifted off the island. Ashley recalls she still didn't know what was going on or why her daughter had seized. Maybe she had meningitis? Maybe it was something else? Nobody knew.

"The next thing I know, we're in an emergency airplane getting transported," she says. "My last memory of this island is that it was pitch black, and I saw lights along the makeshift runway. The lights weren't totally lined up. Later, I learned someone at the hotel had called anyone on the island with a car to go to the tarmac and shine their headlights so our plane could take off. That's been the story of Piper's journey ever since: it gets dark out there, but there's always been a light, even from the very beginning."

Doctors on the mainland originally thought Piper suffered from a classic febrile seizure, but Ashley knew in her gut that it was more than that. When she was eight months old, genetic testing confirmed Piper had Dravet Syndrome, a condition caused by a random genetic mutation in the SCN1A gene. Dravet Syndrome is medication resistant and characterized by frequent and sometimes catastrophic seizures, making it one of the most devastating forms of childhood epilepsies. The loss of oxygen to the brain that occurs during a seizure or cluster dramatically affects the parts of the brain that govern speech, language, and gross motor skills. Because of this, there's a spectrum to Dravet Syndrome, similar to that of autism and Asperger's.

The early conversations with the doctors were, as Ashley puts it, "hell."

"That's where my grief kicked in," she says. "There was no great outlook. It was grim. But my husband and I are doers, fixers. We were trying to get the best care for Piper that we could. We came together in being pushy about the ketogenic diet, which was only offered if patients are older. The hospital didn't have the treatment available for toddlers, but we advocated for it and got it anyway."

Piper had a stable first few years of life following that volatile start. When the keto diet began to fail, though, Ashley recalls dark times. Piper was having twenty to thirty back-to-back grand mal seizures. With these clusters, she was hospitalized every five to six weeks, intubated, and under heavy sedatives. She had no quality of life.

"It was one of the most horrific times in our lives," Ashley recalls. "We almost lost Piper three times. The syndrome goes through their little bodies in a very wild way. For no rhyme or reason, anything would spark her, and we were again left at the mercy of the seizures. I lived in between hope and grief."

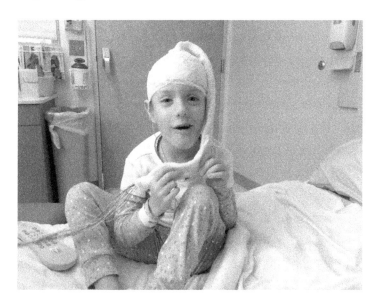

At the time, Tim was pushing hard for Piper to have access to a CBD-based drug, Epidiolex (GW Biosciences), that was headed towards FDA approval (and, as of this writing, received it about a year ago). On January 1, 2014, Piper was the second child in the United States to receive a trial of the drug under the compassionate use clause—and one of the strongest responders.

"She went from clusters of twenty to thirty seizures to seven months of seizure freedom after one dose," Ashley says.

Today, at eleven and a half, Piper's seizures have returned at the rate of about one a week—a rate Ashley knows is still too high. Piper is currently on a cocktail of four drugs, and the family just received confirmation that Piper has been accepted to receive Fintepla (Fenfluramine) via compassionate use: Fintepla (Fenfluramine), a drug that has been used to treat obesity and that has shown incredibly strong response rates in children with Dravet Syndrome.

In addition to these drugs, the family has also pursued other treatments, such as acupuncture and craniosacral therapy. Because sleep disorders often accompany Dravet Syndrome, Piper used to have what Ashley describes as "a lovely healer" come in and play meditative music to help Piper rest—all pro bono.

"You name it, and we're open to it," Ashley says.

Today, Piper is high functioning and fully ambulatory. Her speech and language are delayed, and expressive language has been especially tough for her since seizures affect the muscles in and around the mouth. Piper rides her bike to school with Ashley jogging by her side. Mimi, her twin, is in sixth grade; because Piper needed to repeat kindergarten, she is in fifth and is currently 90 percent efficient at decoding words at a first-grade level.

"It's a big gap, yes," Ashley says. "But as I've witnessed her life with all these seizures, I'm just blown away that she is starting to read. For a while, we thought that may not happen. This summer, we went to an amusement park, and she read a sign that said, 'hot dogs on a stick.' She was just so proud."

Ashley says she and her husband are good at stretching their discomfort, too, encouraging Piper to live her life. Piper rides roller coasters, goes tubing on the water with her brother and sister, and rides boogie boards. When she swims, she can hold her breath for the longest of anyone in the family. She also loves animals, especially horses, and has been riding since she was two years old.

"The biggest thing in her life is that she has a deep connection to the person who helps us care for her," Ashley says. "She's a second mother to Piper. After losing her daughter in a tragic accident, we met when the kids were infants. I had hit my ceiling, and she needed something to do with her heart. Here we are, eleven years later, and Laura is still with us! I am certain she is an angel."

There are, of course, challenges. Piper has a mild to moderate intellectual disability, and the family hopes she will advance as far as fifth-grade reading and development.

"That doesn't mean Tim and I are going to stop," Ashley says. "But it does help us put the brakes on when we need to and helps us not make everything about her development."

Ashley says the couple went through another round of grief recently when they understood that, while their goal is for Piper to be as independent and functional as possible in her adult life, she will always need a person with her. This is because she could have a seizure at any time, but it's also because her judgment and awareness when it comes to safety are simply not there.

"Many of Piper's symptoms have a coexistence with those found in children with autism," Ashley says. "It takes a fair amount of presence and patience. I think modern parenting is crazy-hard in general, and this is that on steroids."

Ashley and Tim have, themselves, been in therapy from the beginning. Ashley, who is a therapist, says she understands the importance of taking this step for them as individuals, as a couple, and as a family unit.

"Stress and freaking out makes things worse," she says. "As I began to apply what I knew as a therapist in my own home, we've found a healthier way to navigate the stress epilepsy brings to families. In my private practice, I now provide care to patients adjusting to epilepsy because I understand epilepsy is a family diagnosis, much like addiction. I also coauthored what's called *Life Support for Families Living with Epilepsy*, which includes practical tools and tips, including how to talk to siblings of epileptic children."

It hasn't always been smooth, though, even with therapy. Sometimes, Ashley says she and Tim will get mad at epilepsy, and they'll take it out on each other. Therapy and communication help ground them—and it doesn't hurt, she says, that they are deeply committed to their partnership.

Even though Ashley professionally supports families

dealing with epilepsy, she admits she struggled in the beginning, especially when it came to Mimi and Owen.

"Even though I had all this knowledge and research, it would all go out of my brain when we were in trauma with Piper," Ashley says. "I'd drop everything with Owen and Mimi, and I wouldn't circle back with them."

The last time they were hospitalized—before Epidiolex—was around Christmas. Owen, eight at the time, saw Tim packing and asked if the whole family could go to the hospital together. In all the commotion, it was something Ashley had never considered.

"We looked at him and Mimi—with Piper seizing every fifteen minutes—and we told them to grab their sleeping bags. That was the turning point when I began to wake up for them," she says.

Soon thereafter, Owen started having panic attacks. Ashley's dear friend and colleague helped Ashley see that this was an opportunity to get him support, and the family started therapy right away. After about a nine-month stretch, Owen's panic attacks had disappeared. Driving home from an appointment, Ashley remembers a conversation she had with her son.

"I don't think I need to do therapy anymore," Owen said. "Do you remember that crazy voice in my head I was so scared of? It wasn't a voice. It was the noise Piper makes when she has a seizure. She was on my back one time when we were playing, and she had a seizure, and the noise got stuck in my head. But now it's not there anymore."

Owen, Ashley says, was the change agent in helping her wake up and face the weight of Piper's diagnosis on the entire family—and they're all better for it.

Once, Ashley went to a healer in a moment of grief. She recalls thinking, "This is not a part of my parenting plan." The healer told her Piper was fine. She said Piper came into the world knowing she'd have this life ahead of her—and so did her sister and brother—and she wanted Ashley to learn how to take care of herself, too. Ashley, a triathlete, tries to do just that—for herself, and also for her family.

"Piper is constantly teaching me," Ashley says. "She's put me on the fast track for the personal growth and transformation I needed. When a seizure hits, it's an instant reset of knowing what is important. It is a reminder that now is a gift. And no, I wouldn't mind if a cure came along for Piper and all kids like her. But, until then, I'm going to take the lesson every day."

"If we listened to the doctors describe the prognosis for Piper ten years ago and look at Piper today, there's no comparison," Ashley says. "She's so full of joy, resiliency, and grit. She wears this cute little soft helmet every day, which is the only reason people know anything is different about her. She can have a seizure that literally knocks her down, she'll pass out, then she'll wake up, and ask to play a game. She's a miracle."

SAMMY'S STORY

TODAY, SAMMY IS SIX YEARS OLD. HE LOVES MUSIC, laughing, and being silly. He enjoys being active, especially going to concerts, visiting playgrounds, and swimming.

Another fact about Sammy, one his parents, Anna and Joey, address as simply another attribute about their son—is that he has Cerebral Palsy (CP) with global delays.

"We don't talk about it as a disability, but rather as just something that's part of him, like having brown hair. You are not a person with brown hair. You are you, and you have brown hair. You may have defining characteristics, but they don't define you wholly as a person," says Anna.

Sometimes, when parents see Sammy crawling on the playground, Joey will explain that his son has CP and can't walk yet. He often hears, "Oh, I'm so sorry."

"If I could change anything about the world around any kind of brain injury diagnosis, I'd say it's not a 'sorry' situation. It's a starting point. Yes, a different starting point than typical children have, but a starting point. They say sorry, which stops their ideas about Sam, relating to him, and seeing him for who he is. They think it's an end point. We never have," Joey says.

One look at Sammy's journey from the beginning proves that.

Anna and Joey knew Sammy had CP when he was just minutes old, due to a brain injury he sustained at birth. After a healthy pregnancy, they had to grapple quickly with a diagnosis they'd never expected. The doctors did tests— brain scans and more—and called a meeting, telling the couple their son would never walk or talk.

"The MRI they showed us was black. They told us there was barely any gray matter. I didn't know what that meant exactly, but they said we were looking at a very disabled child," Joey recalls. "We were trying to be positive, asking what he *would* be able to do. They said, 'maybe a personality.' It was grim and awful."

When Sammy opened his eyes in the NICU, though, he gave his parents a look that told them otherwise.

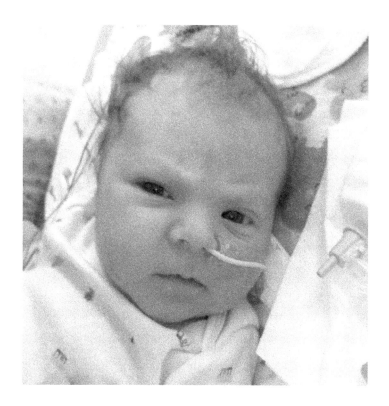

"We could just tell that he was *there*. From that second on, we never doubted who he was. Of course we eventually wanted him to walk and talk. Even then, I knew maybe that wasn't in the cards, and I had to be okay with that too. Life is a hard balance of wanting so much for your kid but accepting who they are at the same time," Anna says.

After he gave his parents that look, Sammy started to do incredible things that were counter to the diagnosis he had been given. For two weeks, the medical team thought Sammy had meningitis. Because it was hard to get the IV in, by the end of the course, they'd started using PIC lines.

Even those weren't working. Anna and Joey—who are both artists—credit the same intuition and sensitivity they use in their craft for allowing them to look at Sammy and see where their child needed to go, despite what they were told.

The couple was not convinced Sammy had meningitis and threatened to leave the hospital. The Head of Disease at the Children's Hospital of Oakland reviewed their case and eventually gave them the okay to leave—but not until Sammy was able to breastfeed, something the doctors never thought he'd do.

Ultimately, the chiropractor Anna had worked with during her pregnancy came to the hospital after the couple sent out a plea for help. He did a small adjustment and some gentle touching, and the newborn latched on right away, proving to the medical team he was able to go home.

Once Sammy came home from the hospital, Anna and Joey leaned into alternative medicines and have remained open to all options—not east or west, but all of it in an integrated fashion—in whatever way most pertains to Sammy's needs at the time. Though many times therapies have been cost prohibitive, the couple has continued to seek out ways to ensure their son gets what he needs.

"It was a long grieving process to come to terms with the diagnosis. It's been delicate because we've never ignored the CP. We've just always looked at Sammy not as a child with CP, but as Sammy. We worked with him. We didn't want to predict the future with our child. Instead, we sought out ideas that pushed all of us forward," Anna says.

One milestone that pushed Sammy forward happened when he was eight months old. Anna had taken him to Whole Foods, and she'd handed him a free magazine. Sammy flipped through and focused on one page: one with information on something called neuromovement, led by a local woman named Anat Baniel. The way it was focused on potential and positivity spoke to both Anna and Joey, and they homed in on the Anat Baniel Method (ABM).

At that point, Sammy wasn't rolling over or moving much. He's been doing ABM—among many other treatments—since that point, and the family has seen substantial advancements in his activity level as well as decreases in the pain and tightness in his limbs.

"We've found a lot of CP kids don't like to be touched or moved, but Sammy likes body work. That's one direct thing we can see in all this—that gentle movement has helped him become aware of his body and have as little pain as possible," Joey says.

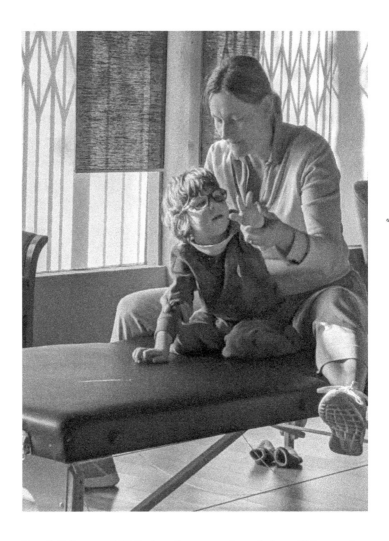

In addition to ABM, they have explored the wilder realm of the Feldenkrais Method—the idea that the brain is more capable of growing and healing than traditionally thought. Sammy has also seen success with acupuncture and chiropractic care. When he was one and a half, the family started a GoFundMe page to help fund hyperbaric oxygen therapy (HBO) for their son, which was quite expensive.

"That [HBO] was a profound experience," Anna recalls. "I would get into the chamber with him. We went five days a week for three months. Before then, he hadn't slept more than two hours at a time. During that time, he started sleeping six to eight hours, growing and recovering from his day! His movement picked up around that time, too."

Sleep has consistently been a challenge for Sammy. Besides HBO, Anna and Joey also incorporate Epsom salt baths, melatonin in juice, and calorie-dense meals full of healthy fats to help him rest.

Today, he has music therapy and swimming on the weekends, which he loves. Sammy also uses Galileo Vibrational Plates in the home, which helps reduce motor development issues, chronic pains, and spasticity while helping muscles grow. He also uses Augmentative and Alternative Communication (AAC) technology, including an iPad with a touch screen to help him communicate. (Joey programs jokes into it for him to tell at school, which Sammy loves!)

"This communication piece has made a huge difference," Anna says. "I've seen, even with our parents, how his and others' perspectives can change. Sammy will participate more because he knows he's being seen, I think."

Sammy feels seen—but what about Anna and Joey? As parents, they say they haven't addressed self-care as much as they could have, pouring all their energy into their son.

For the past four years, while Joey was at work, Anna cared for Sammy. When he got home after his commute, they'd switch. Taking time for themselves has been a struggle that they say they're just now addressing.

"Despite everything we do, there's part of us that is still heartbroken at this experience," Joey says. "How much self-care is going to heal that? But it's a new territory now that Sammy is in school, and we're both trying more. This has been challenging, yes, but it's also made me a better person in the end. It's let me see who he is, not just this idea of who he is, and it's taught me to be present in my own life."

"I struggle with the self-care piece too, but we're working on it," Anna says. "This process has shown me how capable we all are. I see Sammy overcoming these things people said would never happen, and it shows me that if he is capable of that, we are capable of so many things, too. Being Sammy's mom has shifted my ideas of myself and what defines limitations."

Right now, Sammy is trying to walk. Both Joey and Anna admit that he may be trying for a long time, but that's not the focus—if he *does* get there, they say, no matter what, he is going to have to crawl first. And crawling, too, is worth celebrating. The couple has rid themselves of the timelines that are given to children who develop typically and instead focus on what they call "input, input, input" to keep Sammy's brain going, without judging whether it's sticking or if he's "getting it."

For parents facing new challenging medical news for their child, Anna and Joey recommend finding holistically what works for your family and—above all—trust your instincts as much or more as the diagnosis. Anna, in particular, also recommends reading *The Conscious Parent* by Dr. Shefali Tsabary—which is not written especially for moms and dads of differently-abled kids, but instead shows how all parents can be dynamic supporters of their children as they grow and evolve. To that point, the saying, "they give special kids to special parents" is one the couple rebuffs.

"No, we're not special," Anna says. "We're just parents, and this is the kid we have. If we had a different kid, we'd try to be the best parent for *that* kid. Trust yourself and what you know of your child. You don't have to work with people who read your kid's file like a phone book while ignoring the person right in front of them."

Overall, Anna and Joey say they wish people would slow

down a little more—something Sammy has taught them both. They don't know how to be the parents of a typically abled child, they say, but they *do* know that every day, their child is getting older and changing. They love that they're still getting to know him—and they wish others would take a moment too, instead of averting their eyes or offering unwarranted apologies.

"Slow down, stop judging, and communicate with people. Give them a chance. That's how I would like people to approach those with differences. At one point, we're all going to lose part of our abilities—through accident, age, etc.," Anna says. "We're vulnerable to having things happen to us. I'd like to shift the whole conversation around having a disability to say that it's not the end of the line, not a thing to be pitied."

For Anna and Joey, hope like this is not an idea—it is a tool. It is, as they describe, "a religion" in their household. To this day, doctors will still sometimes tell them they're in denial.

"Ok, he may never talk. Or he may only have one word. I don't know. But I'm going to keep trying, offering him things, and seeing and appreciating what he *is* doing and *who* he is," Anna says.

Once, a doctor explained they didn't want to offer the couple "false hope"—which did not sit well. Anna and Joey say they don't believe there is such thing as false hope; there is, instead, just hope.

"If you have hope, you have the tenacity to keep going.

That's one thing that you need as a special needs parent. To learn to accept who your child is and that their life will improve in many ways. Their circle of friends will grow. They will get to play. They will get to go to the beach. Just... life. They will have that."

LAIRD'S STORY

TODAY, MELISSA MURFEY DESCRIBES HER SON LAIRD as eleven-going-on-twenty-five. He's bright, hysterically funny, and is very active—skiing, surfing, biking, and participating in runs. He's also into music and is working with a producer in Los Angeles to move one of his songwriting projects forward. He enjoys playing with his older brother Carl and his younger brother Ryder, and they bicker just as brothers do.

Oh, and one more thing: Laird has cerebral palsy. He uses a wheelchair, and he cannot use his hands or talk (though he uses technology to communicate—which he has mastered). When he was born, Melissa's uterus ruptured, and Laid spent forty minutes without oxygen before the doctors got him out. He was diagnosed with hypoxic-ischemic encephalopathy (HIE) at birth. Laird spent thirty days in the NICU, and Melissa recalls the back-and-forth of tending to both her sick newborn and her other son at home, twenty-month-old Carl.

"When a child is born with something as severe as a brain injury, your brain goes into fight or flight. We just wanted him home," Melissa says. "When he finally got home, I was thinking, 'This is a good run of time for us because he's not missing any milestones. He's doing everything a one-month old does.'"

At three years old, Laird was diagnosed with cerebral palsy.

A lot happened during that time—and after. At birth, Melissa and Scott had banked Laird's cord blood, and they began stem cell transfusions as early as possible thanks to the compassionate use protocol. Besides transfusions, they also learned all they could about neuroplasticity and pursued Masgutova Neurosensory Reflex Integration and the Feldenkrais method early on. Melissa credits The Family Hope Center, a support and resource center in Pennsylvania, for giving the family ideas and direction. It wasn't long before they were pursuing the Anat Baniel Method (ABM) as well, taking Laird to Marin County, California, for therapy at the Anat Baniel Center almost one hundred days of the year, on average.

"We knew the brain is still developing up to age five, and we tried to get as much going as we could because we didn't have a great prognosis," Melissa recalls. "No one fully understands what the brain is capable of. We just didn't want to hedge our bets and miss out on any time."

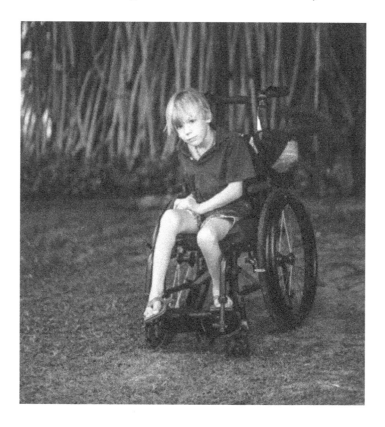

Before the treatments, Laird was fragile when it came to anything sensory. He was also highly spastic. After treatments, he "went more on the floppy side, and his sensory stuff calmed down," Melissa says. Because they tried so many treatments and therapies, she's not sure which one attributed most to Laird's improvement.

"We tried so many things all at once, just input-input-input," she says. "It's impossible to tell what is responsible for what. We were just lucky to have the means to try everything. I know that's not common, and we are grateful to have had the access we did."

Today, Melissa and Scott's sons continue to grow physically, emotionally, and socially. The social piece is particularly interesting, she says, because so far, the social situations have been trickier for Laird's brothers than him.

"They can be known as 'the brother of the kid in a wheelchair,'" she says. "But the dynamics are constantly changing. We walk the line between being hopeful and answering questions that will not lead to crushed expectations later. When Laird asks me how he will propose to his wife one day, for example, I'm not sure how to respond to that. I'm not sure there is a right answer."

If she were to give advice to parents just starting their journey post-diagnosis, Melissa says she would refer parents to The Family Hope Center first. She also recommends getting on the same page with your spouse or partner about your approach and goals so that you can tackle obstacles together. She also found it helpful to connect with a parent who has a child with the same condition, but who is older. That way, Melissa says, you can see and learn from experiences before you face them, and you can have a person with whom you connect to bounce ideas off of.

That said, the most important recommendation, according to Melissa, is not one of action but one of attitude.

"You can get stuck in the hard part of it all and turn everything into a pity party," she says. "I don't do that. Yes, of course there was grief. Of course it's hard. But we don't let any of that stop us. We choose to live in what is possible and what we can do. Every day, we go full steam ahead. We know how lucky we are."

ASHLEY'S STORY

WHEN JANE'S OLDEST DAUGHTER, ASHLEY, WAS JUST
over three-and-a-half years old, she was diagnosed with
leukemia. Before that point, she'd been healthy and
developing neurotypically. The news was, of course, devastating—and made even more challenging when they soon
learned Ashley had a subtype of leukemia, hypodiploid
acute lymphoblastic leukemia, that affects only 1 percent
of patients. Because chemo won't kill that type of cancer,

they knew they had one option: a bone marrow transplant. They searched internationally for a match (Ashley is half Korean and half Chinese) but could not find a donor.

"We didn't have that much time," Jane says. "We had to go to Plan B and participate in a clinical trial that allowed someone who is half a match to be the donor, and by definition, parents are half a match."

Jane was Ashley's donor, and the procedure was a success, putting the then four-year-old in remission. Then came another problem: after a bone marrow transplant, most patients are left without an immune system for about six months. In Ashley's case, hers took fifteen months to recover. During that time, she contracted the Epstein-Barr virus (EBV)—and it went right to her brain.

They didn't know at first that EBV was the cause of Ashley's lethargy and fevers. After a couple weeks, Jane took her daughter into the hospital for examination, but they were soon discharged. They went back three days later, when Ashley would not wake up or eat. Jane knew something was wrong.

"They told us maybe it was something neurological," Jane recalls. "Then, the spinal fluid results came back positive for EBV. It penetrated the blood-brain barrier really quickly. They gave her medication to decrease the EBV, but the symptoms just got worse and worse."

Within six weeks of arriving at the hospital, Ashley had to be transferred to the PICU because the pressure in her brain (Intracranial Pressure, or ICP) became so high, and subsequent MRIs showed the brain damage was getting worse.

"They told us we had three options. We could try a little bit of radiation, give her more EBV fighting medication, or keep her comfortable in case nothing worked," Jane recalls. "That was not something my husband and I were expecting at that point. When the social worker mentioned different ways we could keep her comfortable, I started envisioning her funeral. Should we ask guests to attend the service wearing her favorite colors, pink and purple? Or should we opt for the traditional black? But I had to quickly stop going down that rabbit hole because I had to stay strong for Ashley."

The family opted for radiation, but not the high dosage many recommended. Their radiologist found a study that showed a three-day course, as opposed to the two-week course that could have left their daughter in a vegetative state, might work.

"They told us if the three-day didn't work, we'd have to do the two-week. And if that didn't work, we'd have to let her go," Jane says.

It worked! After a sixth-month long hospitalization to treat her, Ashley got to go home with her family. The neurologist advised Jane and her husband to follow traditional treatments, telling them because Ashley was so young and her brain still spastic, she would "be fine."

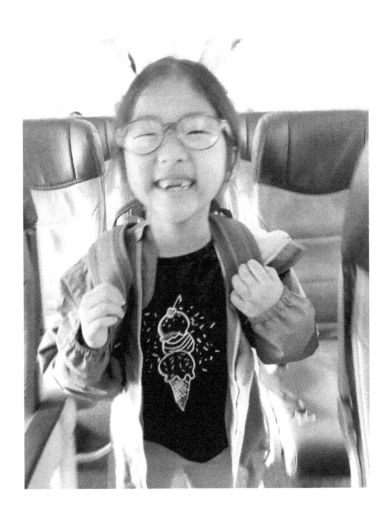

Ashley did as much PT, OT, and speech therapy as possible once home. Jane and her husband have continued to pursue treatments to help their daughter, including Masgutova Neurosensorimotor Reflex Integration (MNRI), aqua therapy, music therapy, Hyperbaric Oxygen Therapy (HBOT), vision therapy, and more. MNRI and music therapy have been especially helpful, Jane says, because of Ashley's love of music and her improvement with eye tracking and fine motor coordination.

Before kindergarten started, Jane and her husband worked hard to get their daughter a 1:1 aid and followed every recommendation they could find. They were still hopeful Ashley would return to who she was pre-brain injury.

Today, Ashley is seven and a half. Because of her severe acquired brain injury, she has cortical vision impairment, speech and language impairment, dyslexia, and social, developmental, and emotional delays. Because most of her brain injury was on her left side, she has right-sided weakness.

"The physical stuff doesn't bother me as much as the cognitive stuff," Jane says. "We truly thought she was going to recover cognitively. This past year, in the first grade, we realized it wasn't going to be that way."

The couple came to this realization after meeting with a neuropsychologist who did a full exam on Ashley last summer. She took her MRIs and academic testing together to give the family a view of who Ashley is now and who she may be in the future.

After hearing so many times before that Ashley's brain would rewire itself and "figure it out," the couple got an explanation of what global damage to both white and gray matter means. They were told Ashley should be in an academic environment that encourages functional skills.

"That was the turning point for me," Jane says. "Of

course, I knew the brain injury was significant. I didn't know that what was damaged would hinder what she's able to learn in the future. That conversation was sobering. Still, I was not and still am not ready to accept that IQ. I know it's just a number, but I feel like with the right academic setting and treatments, she will learn how to read, do basic math, and live semi-independently. That's where I am right now."

Over the last six months, Jane says she and her husband have been going through the process of grieving the "old Ashley."

"We now know that she will have special needs indefinitely, so we're focusing on how to give her a fulfilling life. It has been a transition, and it's been heartbreaking," Jane says. "It's hard because a lot of times we don't know what she's thinking, but of course she has feelings like the rest of us. Anything that would make a neurotypical child sad— like not being included, or not being able to play a game because it's too difficult—makes her sad, too."

While she has her tough moments, Ashley's overall demeanor is one of total joy. Jane says her teachers and therapists love working with her, especially because she's so encouraging.

"She'll yell, 'you can do it daddy!' when he's opening a can," Jane says. "Or she'll clap after the teacher gives a lesson."

Today, Ashley's primary challenges are poor attention, memory, and cortical vision impairment. Ashley's short attention span makes it very difficult for her to learn. The doctors say the poor attention is a direct result of her brain injury, and when she needs a break, her brain is truly unable to keep going. Though they've had some success, finding the right treatments has been a struggle. Jane says she sometimes feels she "is in a black hole trying to find treatments and products to help Ashley."

Focusing so much on Ashley—as well as her sister Lauren and her younger brother Jason—means Jane doesn't have a lot of time to herself. She says she's met a few moms along this journey, and when it comes to self-care, each mom needs something different.

For Jane, in the first couple of years, it was hard to give herself a break. She recalls she'd get a workout in to release endorphins. More recently now that things are stable, she's starting to invest in real estate, something she can do on her own time that's exciting. For any new moms facing a troubling diagnosis, Jane encourages them to figure out what makes them happy and find time for a little break.

"But I get it," Jane says. "It's so tough. You're always thinking of your kids. For me, one of the hardest parts is knowing Jason [who just turned one] will never know who Ashley was before. And it took a couple of years for Lauren to realize she wasn't going to have the same big sister she had before Ashley got sick. Even with all of that, the Ashley we have today is still so full of joy and is such a great big sister. We consider ourselves lucky."

SOSKAY'S STORY

WHEN AKIHO MATSUNAGA WAS PREGNANT WITH HER son, Soskay, the doctors knew early on that he had medical issues. They suspected Trichosemy-18 or Down syndrome; an amniocentesis affirmed the latter.

Akiho, who had worked with preschool and daycare-aged children with Down syndrome, knew she had a special child coming her way. Still, she didn't feel ready. Together with her husband Junichi, they had many genetic counseling visits.

"We still did not know what was best for us and the baby," she says.

Then, doctors confirmed that devastatingly, Soskay also had a heart defect, and an obvious one at that.

"Doctors weren't sure if he would survive long after he was born," Akiho recalls. "But I knew we would follow this baby and support him in whatever he needed."

When Soskay was born on January 23, 2010, he was immediately transferred to a specialty children's hospital. He had a tricuspid valve leakage, which means that one valve was not closing properly, causing the blood to go backwards. In short, his heart wasn't getting enough oxygen. On top of that, he had lung issues and a liver hemangioma, so the blood was going to his liver and creating a tumor.

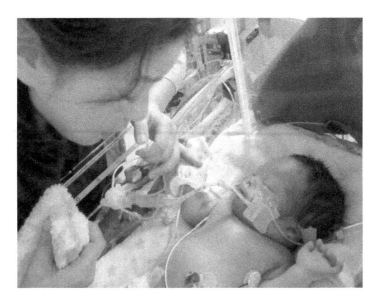

With Soskay intubated, the doctors told his parents he would need high-risk surgery, the scope of which may change once they were in the room and had to make quick decisions.

"We told the doctors to come out and tell us what was going on step-by-step so we could decide what to do," Akiho recalls. "Luckily, on the first try, it worked. He spent six more weeks in ICU after that before he came home."

With Soskay home, Akiho tried feeding him. She recalls giving him one sip of milk, and after that, he fell asleep for six hours. When he awoke, his face was blue. She also noted his head was bobbing. She took him to a cardiologist; two days later, the family found out he didn't have enough oxygen. Soskay was airlifted back to the children's hospital, where he was transferred to the ICU with heart failure.

"They told me he had one or two days," Akiho recalls. "And that's it. The doctors said there was nothing else they could do besides just treat his hemangioma."

They referred the family to Canuck Place, a children's hospice in British Columbia. Akiho says that's not what the family wanted at the time; they just wanted Soskay home.

"We had conversations with the doctors, and they didn't seem to understand our wishes," she says. "They thought we needed to have a translator to understand, but we didn't. We did understand. We just wanted to take our baby home."

Finally, after a translator confirmed that it wasn't the family who needed a translator, but it was, in fact, the doctors—two nurses fully supported them in their decision. Finally, they took their child home.

"We thought, every day, let's support Soskay fully. Let's make memories as much as possible," she says. "Until that day, I hadn't even bought a lot of things for him because I knew he might not make it. After that, we got him things—decorations, a kimono, a warrior helmet. We took his handprints and footprints. All the things you do to celebrate a baby."

At the time, Soskay required 24/7 care, which the family provided. It took a toll on them.

"At first, we were overwhelmed. We felt like we couldn't smile anymore because we'd lost hope for how our family would be. We worried about our two-and-a-half-year-old daughter, Nana, and how she felt."

Still, the Matsunaga family stayed strong.

"We want the best for him," Akiho says. "We did physio-therapy, occupational therapy, speech. Today, we take him to the Down Syndrome Research Foundation, a two-hour trip from where we live. Whatever we have available, I tap into those resources."

Soskay stopped requiring oxygen when he was two years old. Still, one thing was tethering him; one resource the Matsunaga family desperately wanted to find was one that would help wean Soskay off of his feeding tube.

"They told us it was dangerous to take him off, and the pediatrician said he needed to be on it for another five years," Akiho says. "He'd been on one since birth. We did all the tests they recommended, and we just couldn't see why he needed to be on one still."

One day, when trying to find new resources, Akiho typed in the words "tube dependency" into the search bar. She found a feeding tube weaning program called NoTube. The program, based in Australia, provides online consultation and support. Akiho recalls being so impressed by how just knowing what to search for can change your access to information.

The doctors, though, weren't so sure.

"Soskay's complex feeding team said if I did NoTube, they would not support me. I went to a new pediatrician, who said he didn't know about the weaning program but would help us along the way. But we needed to make a decision."

"A month after we started, he wasn't taking formula in the tube. Two months after, he was off fluids altogether in the tube. Three months after, he wasn't using the tube at all," she recalls. "It was life changing for us, going from a twenty-four-hour tube that almost controlled our life to now having our son in a more free state. If we didn't pursue NoTube, I think he would still be on it now, and we wouldn't be where we are today."

It hasn't always been easy, Akiho says, but it's always been worth it.

"Now, we know we are not alone," she recalls. "So many people created space for us as a family. At the hospital and when we do visit Canuck Place now—which has just been so incredible—we've met other families and shared our stories. We feel less alone, especially because we are away from our own families in Japan."

Medically, Soskay is doing well living with his unique heart condition. He's not a candidate for a transplant because his body has defied odds and is working with his abnormal heart; the doctors don't think he would survive a transplant.

"His heart isn't fixed. It's still leaking," Akiho says. "Nobody knows why it's working. It's a miracle. So, we enjoy Soskay every day, and he teaches us so many things. Before he was born, I hesitated a little to have a special needs child—not because I wouldn't love him, of course, but because I wanted him to have a good life and a place in this world. Because of the people I've met and where we are today, I don't wonder that anymore. He has a place."

RYAN'S STORY

"YES, HE IS BEHIND, BUT HE CAN STILL READ. LET'S wait and see."

"Yes, he has attention challenges, but he's a boy. He just needs to run it off. Let's wait and see."

These are the comments Allison heard from teachers about her son, Ryan (now almost thirteen), many times before he received his actual diagnosis: dyslexia. Although that diagnosis didn't come until recently, Allison knew something was wrong long ago, back when she worked with Hooked on Phonics with Ryan just as she had her older son, Josh. Ryan didn't catch on as quickly and started missing official benchmarks beginning in kindergarten.

It wasn't just reading, comprehension, and writing. Like autism, dyslexia has a spectrum. For Ryan, the condition also manifests in attention issues, memory challenges, and struggles with disorganized thinking.

The "wait and see approach" didn't work so well, despite meeting after meeting at the school. One day, Ryan's third grade teacher—a friend Allison had gone to high school with—pulled Allison aside and said her son needed additional help and testing.

"If she hadn't done that, I don't know what would have happened," Allison recalls. "Nothing against the teachers at all, but I think I was naïve in the fact that I thought the school district would just help him since he was struggling. That wasn't the case."

Ryan was tested through the school and, starting in fourth grade, was given an IEP for what they then termed as a "general reading disability," as schools sometimes hesitate to offer specific diagnoses. Even with school intervention, Ryan still struggled. What would take the 'average' student half an hour to do would take him two and a half hours, at best.

"Everything was longer, harder," Allison says. "We had a lot of tears, a lot of frustration. Ryan is a big boy with a super sweet demeanor. That got him through a lot. A lot of kids would turn to being naughty in these cases, but he has always been gentle and has avoided trouble. To his credit, he basically charmed his way up to the sixth grade."

It was during that sixth grade year that things started to go downhill for Ryan grade-wise. He was no longer passing. That's when Allison decided to seek extra help for her son outside school—and when they got the dyslexia diagnosis.

"Ryan was discouraged, to say the least, before we found out what was going on," Allison says. "We'd spend hours studying, and he'd know the information. Then, he'd take the test and get a thirty. Nobody likes to get a thirty, especially a kid who is a people pleaser."

After he spent six hours with the psychologist and got

the diagnosis, Allison says Ryan became hopeful that there were ways to help him. And that has started to materialize into reality—but the road hasn't been without its bumps.

"I knew nothing about it [dyslexia] then," Allison says. "But I learned it presents itself out of school, which explained so much. It's an executive functioning issue. Ryan is messy. His brain can't do sequences. He can tell you the days of the week, but not the order. If I give him three things to do, even though he tries, I'll be lucky if he can remember one."

The tutor the family hired post-diagnosis teaches Ryan using the Orton-Gillingham Approach, a language-based teaching method developed to help those with dyslexia learn. That approach is not taught in Ryan's normal school, however, so the gap can present a challenge. In addition, the tutor recommended Allison let Ryan read what he enjoyed, so he does. There is one problem, though: other kids have made fun of his "'baby books,'" saying things like, "I read Captain Underpants back when I was in second grade!"

That teasing has affected Ryan. So have the school lessons he struggles to grasp.

Allison works to build Ryan's self-confidence in his schoolwork, encouraging him to raise his hand in class when he doesn't understand something. She heartbreakingly recalls how he told her he simply couldn't—he said he'd be raising his hand all the time.

"Nobody wants to feel 'stupid.' I've learned dyslexia can make you appear like you're not smart—like you can't spell, read, or be organized. Like you're lazy, forgetful, and unmotivated. Like you can't ever find the right words," Allison says. "But my son is a problem solver, great at numbers, puzzles, and visuals. He's very smart."

Allison says that like many with dyslexia, Ryan has developed strategies to get around his reading challenges. Because he was diagnosed later than some, though, part of his treatment may be undoing some of those strategies—or learning to work with them. The family is still discovering the best way.

After Ryan's diagnosis, besides the tutor, Allison also got an advocate to help the family navigate their world through this revised lens—some of which they found more complicated than they expected. For example, the initial report from the psychologist with the diagnosis was seventeen pages.

"It was just a jumble of words I didn't know, but this was something I needed to understand," she recalls.

The advocate made her a CliffsNotes version of the report and explained what was going on and what the recommendation was to help. She also helped Allison write a letter to the school regarding Ryan's IEP—which hadn't changed much as a result of the diagnosis—about how the teachers and staff could best support him. The advocate is also the person who encouraged Allison to pursue medication for her son after his diagnosis of ADHD, inattentive type.

"Meds weren't our first choice," Allison says. "But we knew he had attention issues, and we knew we had to help him. The advocate was really helpful in this aspect because, as a parent, you can be very emotional about your child. She helped us break it all down."

Besides the advocate and tutor, the family has also found technology helpful. There are audiobooks, for example, and Ryan is able to use the speech-to-text feature on the laptop. Allison also made sure the school put in his IEP that Ryan could use his iPad to take a photo of the whiteboard when it lists assignments to avoid instructions getting lost in translation.

Outside of technology, they also use old-fashioned reminders, keeping pen and paper all over the house.

"We believe—and we tell Ryan all the time—that this whole thing is not about labels. It's about helping him succeed," Allison says. "We always tell him that it's not about being smart, it's about how his brain is working. We know this is not something that is ever going to go away, but it is something we can work with. It's about developing strategies to help him live his life."

From a parenting perspective, Allison says that being Ryan's mom requires "so much patience." If they watch a television show as a family, for example, they need to pause it every five minutes because Ryan's brain just can't keep up with the plot. This doesn't feel disruptive, though; it's simply their reality. She also finds herself interacting more with Ryan's teachers, making sure they're up to speed on what's going on with Ryan and how he learns best.

Allison's advice to other parents who may have a child

struggling is clear: trust your instincts, and don't put all your faith in the school system to handle it.

"I knew there was something wrong since preschool, but they just kept telling me to wait and see," Allison says. "There were opportunities for early intervention that we missed. Again, nothing against teachers or the school, but if I could go back, I'd say, 'No, let's take care of this now.'"

Allison wants the world to know that Ryan is not only smart, but he is also brave. If you give him a minute, he will find the answer to whatever is in front of him—but that requires a level of patience, kindness, and understanding we would all be better served to cultivate a little more of.

"Kids who face challenges like this are my definition of brave," Allison says. "I have a little saying about this that I read to Ryan sometimes. It's important to tell him this because when you're in school, being different isn't good. Sometimes, it's hard to face the world with what you've been given. That takes courage."

Allison says that even though it hasn't been that long since they were given the diagnosis and subsequent plan to help her son, Ryan is already doing better.

"He's more encouraged every day to work harder because he knows we see him for who he is: a kid who is trying, a kid who is smart, a kid who we are so proud of every day."

EVELYN'S STORY

WHEN KATIE WAS THIRTY-NINE WEEKS PREGNANT, she stopped feeling her daughter, Evelyn, move. Things took a scary turn from there.

When she arrived at the hospital, the doctors rushed Katie in for an emergency C-section. She wasn't able to be awake for it, as the epidural didn't take. It happened so quickly that even her husband, Adam, couldn't make it in time.

The team of doctors would later tell Katie that Evelyn wasn't breathing when she was born. They had to go to extreme measures to save her life.

"We're still scratching our heads about what happened," Katie says.

Immediately after Evelyn was born, she was transferred to another NICU. There, she had her first seizures. They put her on a cooling pad to help stop the inflammation from spreading. Evelyn was on the cooling pad for four days— four excruciating days, Katie says, because she couldn't hold her daughter.

An MRI taken at six days old showed Evelyn had a significant brain injury, Hypoxic-Ischemic Encephalopathy (HIE).

"It rocked our world," Katie says. "We were in the NICU for eleven days, because it looked like the inflammation to her brain had stopped. It was amazing to go home that soon, and we were incredibly grateful to get out of there. The NICU in itself is a trauma."

Evelyn was discharged with one seizure medication. Over the coming months, she received two additional diagnoses: Microcephaly (a small head) and Cortical Visual Impairment (when the brain doesn't communicate what the eyes are seeing).

Katie recalls asking the medical team what she could do for her daughter.

"The doctor who discharged us told me that if I looked up her condition—HIE—I would find so many scary things.

He said not to do any research, to just do what the medical team said and wait to see what happened. I am a literal person, so I didn't do any research that first year. I wish I had known there was a different way."

Evelyn didn't have any seizures that first year. There were some delays, but she was crawling, rolling over, and starting to babble. At that point, Katie and Adam had hoped to wean her off of the seizure medication. (Katie is quick to point out that she's not anti-medication, but it just made her nervous that her daughter was on a drug that was so powerful, yet they had no knowledge of what the long-term side effects could be.)

Katie, Adam, and Evelyn traveled to Dartmouth in early January 2019 for the EEG—one that would prove to be another turning point in Evelyn's journey.

Katie recalls the technician talking to the couple the whole time, saying there was no evidence of seizures. They left the test feeling positive and hopeful.

They got a call a couple days later: the EEG showed "abnormal brain injury," and the doctor had decided not only to keep Evelyn on the seizure medication, but also to increase the dosage.

That was January 10, 2019—the day Katie knew there had to be more out there.

She called a biomedical doctor at the Biomedical Center of New England, with whom she connected immediately. He recommended Evelyn get started on a few things: chiropractic care (something they'd already been doing), a special diet, craniosacral therapy, and neurological reorganization.

It wasn't their first foray into therapies for Evelyn, by any means. Prior to the call with the biomedical doctor, Katie and Adam had their daughter in typical, state-funded therapy. Katie found it more frustrating than helpful.

"The therapist would tell me what she should be doing—stacking blocks, waving goodbye—but she wasn't telling me how to get her there. I'd go home and practice for hours with what they told me, but nothing was working. I was very discouraged and depressed. I'm thankful we got through it."

Since they began the additional therapies, Katie says, "We've had a huge year. I can't even comprehend how much we've done."

Even so, a seizure in May 2019 came out of the blue.

"It was terrifying. At the hospital, they told me she was still seizing. I didn't realize that's what seizures looked like. She didn't fall on the ground or have rapid shaking. It was subtle. I had NICU flashbacks during that hospital stay. When they were doing rounds, I told them I didn't want to hear what they had to say—I didn't want to hear about 'my brain-injured daughter' anymore. I just wanted my baby home."

Though entirely unexpected, Katie does think she knows what may have contributed to it. Evelyn had a craniosacral therapy session two days before, during which the therapist told her she'd "'had a really big movement.'" It was likely that the body was trying to flush out all the toxins.

"That was a low point for us this year. I went into a kind of downward spiral. I started counseling, and I know I ate too much ice cream. I pulled myself out of it, though. I started doing craniosacral therapy for myself, and I have faith in God. He is my stabilizing hope. I also know that on the road to healing, you have ups and downs, twists and turns. And I wouldn't ever call Evelyn's seizure a good thing, but we have seen a jump since then—in her gains in vision, sensory stimulation, and so much more."

As of this writing, Evelyn is almost two-and-a-half. She goes to craniosacral therapy once a week. There, the therapist begins by working on her diaphragm, because trauma is usually retained in the visceral area of the body. The therapist will listen for a flow and keep pulsing with her hands as she moves, sometimes to the feet or upper back or neck. Then, she goes to the forehead area and the top of the skull, repeating the process.

"I've had it done, too. Especially when she's [the therapist is] touching the top of my head, it feels like she's gently moving the skull bone back and forth, and you can feel this flow in your head. You feel a little dizzy and maybe a little crazy. But, you can feel the freedom of the flowing of the cranial fluid. It encourages the release of trauma and tension and helps your body heal. It's expensive, but it has been worth it for us."

Another cornerstone of Evelyn's progress is neurological reorganization, also called neurodevelopmental therapy. The point of the therapy is to give the injured brain tissue a chance to have a healthy first developmental year. Katie says this, in particular, has been life changing.

"When we go to therapy, it is me, my husband, my mom, and the therapist, and we all move Evelyn in different patterns—for Evelyn, those patterns imitate what a child does in utero, because that's where her TBI was sustained. The whole point is to give the child a healthy start and set up the brain for the rest of the child's life: how they emotionally connect, how they physically move their body, how they respond visually, etc. Evelyn is set to graduate within a year, but it all depends on how the child responds. I told the therapist we'd do it for ten years if we needed to, because that's how much it is helping."

Katie has found a community for herself through the program, too. She's met many other parents—some whose children have TBIs, some whose children have Autism, and so on—and they've connected in person and through a Facebook support group.

Today, Evelyn continues to progress. Katie says she's bonding more with people, understanding more, learning the alphabet, and even how to read, and her vision has improved, too. She wears glasses with a special prism that helps her look straight ahead or even up. It is, as she says, "night and day" from a year ago.

Retrospectively, Katie says advocating for her daughter is and has been her focus.

"I encourage everyone to ask questions, research, and push further," she says. "It's okay to be strong, and you don't have to worry about offending anyone. You can make the phone calls yourself. You don't have to wait and see."

Katie finds it important to take care of herself, too, along this journey.

"I spent a whole year reading Psalms and realizing it's okay to be brokenhearted and angry. I realized God could take my anger, my terror, and my trauma. Giving it to God was one of the biggest things I did. I also turned to meditation and yoga. And I started paying someone to come clean our house. My husband and I are not loaded by any means, but this was a big stress relief for me. I couldn't keep up with the mess. Now, I know that at least once a week, I will have the feeling that everything is in order and my home is peaceful. A clean house does that for me. For another mom, that stress relief could be something else—but I recommend asking for the help you need."

Katie says Evelyn has been a fighter from the get-go. Together, they're ready to face whatever life throws at them.

"I know life is really fragile. My sister-in-law recently lost a baby who was thirty-four weeks along. When I hear stories like that, I realize how much Evelyn is a miracle. That could have been my daughter. Life is such a gift and I feel like everyone on Earth has a chance. I'm really thankful I get to be on Evelyn's journey with her."

CADEN'S STORY

CADEN IS TRULY A UNIQUE FIFTEEN-YEAR-OLD BOY, in the most literal sense of the word: he has no diagnosis, and there is nobody like him in the world. What makes him special transcends far beyond the medical world, though: he also has a passion for music, horses, and the cooking show *Barefoot Contessa*, starring Ina Garten, (who has been his Halloween costume of choice two years running). Simply put, he is a joy. A light.

But let's start at the beginning.

After a smooth pregnancy and birth, the doctors found Caden had meconium in his lungs, which was cleared immediately. The first of his symphony of symptoms surfaced when he failed his newborn hearing test.

His father Noah remembers how traumatic that first bit of news was—that something was less than perfect in his beautiful newborn child.

In his early years, Caden had bad reflux and a hard time holding food down, which made him uncomfortable. He grew slowly and didn't walk until he was around eighteen months (twice the age his older brother learned). During that time, he was diagnosed with vision issues due to severe strabismus, and his family learned he had almost no depth perception. As time progressed, it became increasingly clear that this otherwise charming, happy baby was confronted with many challenges.

All told, the first five years of Caden's life were the hardest for his family—confronting his newly discovered challenges, taking him to three to five doctors' appointments a week, and coming to grips with the reality that their child had undiagnosed limitations. Caden was lucky in that he had an engaged medical team and providers. Still, Noah recalls that the more everyone tried to diagnose and understand his deficits, the more confusing things became. In addition, like many families who have children who are differently-abled, Caden's family went through a divorce when he was around three years of age. This was devastating for both him and his brother. For children who are differently-abled and rely on a predictable structure, such a change can be especially disruptive—as was the case here.

From an early age, Caden gravitated toward adults because he didn't know how to play or communicate with other children. His language skills developed very late and, Noah says, are still evolving to this day. In fact, when he was young, he had very few words, and people had a difficult time understanding him. There's irony here, too: despite his verbal challenges, he excelled at communicating and bonding. Noah says it was clear from the start that there was much more going on inside his son than could be identified.

This holds true fifteen years later—and, in many ways, he remains the same mystery of unexpected wonders. Caden has been remarkably resilient in his ability to form relationships and bonds with others. Noah says this has been his great gift that seems to get him what he needs while filling the hearts of those he wins over.

Caden's life was once again changed forever when he met his beloved Patti, who would become his stepmother, at the age of eight. They had an instant, kindred spirit bond. He has always had people who care about him, but the bond with Patti was, and is, unique. Then and to this day, she engages him on every level, sees the joy in Caden versus the struggle, and gives him tremendous unconditional love. Given Caden's powers of connection, he knew he had found someone worth holding onto.

Caden is a lucky boy in that he has two families who love and care for him, each offering different unique experiences. His stepfather, Gary, often takes him to baseball games, on the ferry, or boating with friends. His mother, Laura, has begun taking him to the gym at 5:00 in the morning. Much to his brother's embarrassment, he likes to go from machine to machine, talking to people. Caden is surrounded by family, extended family, and a broad network of friends between the two households, giving him rich and varied experiences. The back and forth between households can indeed be disruptive at times, but it also gives both sets of families a break and the opportunity to miss Caden. Plus, he gets more stimulation and love than he would from one family.

Today, Caden has two families who work collaboratively and cooperatively to do what's best for him. The adults in his life have learned to put aside their personal issues, needs, and resentments—all for Caden's best interest. Of course, Noah admits, there are challenges in having two different households. But he says his son has been an exceptional teacher, forcing his two sets of parents to continually grow and collaborate for a higher purpose.

Diagnosis-wise (or lack thereof), Caden has mild cerebral palsy as well as symptoms commonly found in autism, such as developmental and language delays. He also has high-frequency hearing loss, vision issues, and an intellectual disability as a result of genetic abnormalities that occurred in utero.

His list of symptoms is long, but his diagnosis is short: his case is so rare that he doesn't technically have one. For this reason, finding what works for Caden is something

Patti and Noah refer to as "an ongoing process," having pursued "every treatment option under the sun, from speech, to occupational, to physical." They play it day by day, month by month, and year by year when it comes to understanding his true capabilities and what is possible for his future.

Outside of medical terms, Caden is far easier to diagnose: He has laughter. He has an exceptionally high level of emotional intelligence. He has a strong will and an independent spirit. He has a desire to be around and connect with people. He has happiness.

Patti and Noah feel that while a diagnosis for Caden would have alleviated some of the unnecessary worries and perhaps created a "road map" for raising such an extraordinary child, in the end, it probably would not have changed much. Each child has their own unique needs and demands. It makes a certain amount of sense to them, then, that a child whose brain works differently would have their own unique needs.

Treatment-wise, the one technique Patti and Noah have found that has been the most effective for Caden's progress is social interaction. This has been positive because Caden has always wanted to be included, and he simply loves people. Once, Patti and Noah lost sight of him in a crowded store for merely a few moments, only to find him riding back to them on the front of a smiling elderly woman's motorized cart. This was no surprise to the family, as he is drawn to anyone with gray hair, calling them "mee-maw." This fluidity with people extends into the classroom, where he is currently thriving with friends and a teacher both parents agree are "angels on earth."

There have been some bumps along the way. As Caden has grown into a teenager, he—like many kids—hasn't always loved being told what to do. Because he's not always able to find language to express himself, discontent or frustration often manifests into aggression. At the school he attended prior to this one (which wasn't so good a fit), educators suggested medication to modify behavior—something Patti and Noah felt may dampen their son's energetic personality. Thankfully, the episodes are fewer and farther between as of this writing, and they've worked through them as a family.

As Caden grows up, he wants to become more independent, which Patti and Noah wholeheartedly encourage. He has an adult tricycle he rides around the neighborhood, his dad by his side. He also runs errands with Patti often. Once, Patti recalls having to drop off a package at the UPS Store. There was little parking, so she asked Caden to take the box inside the store for her. He was nervous at first, making sure she was going to watch him. Once assured, he went inside and completed the task all on his own. Patti still remembers the pride on his face when he returned, beaming and reaching in to hug her through the car window.

Ultimately, what independence will look like down the road is still up in the air for the family. Sometimes, when Patti travels for work, Caden will sit by the door for hours at a time, waiting for her to return. Their attachment—and love—runs deep. Understandably, the couple also have independence questions of their own: As they get older, what about their independence? What will retirement look like? What about the financial side of support, which can feel worrisome? This topic was recently top of mind for the family after insurance declined to pay for additional OT, stating it was no longer effective. On one hand, the refusal was hard to hear for Patti, as she felt it was like the company was giving up on her child, and she was left to wonder if maybe this really was the best it was going to get physically.

Noah, on the other hand, tended to agree with the decision; even though Caden can't button a shirt or tie his shoelaces, he can still dress himself. That's progress, and moving on to Noah meant energy to focus elsewhere—elsewhere, that is, into a context in which his son could continue to learn.

All in all, the experience is an emotional roller coaster for the family. What's hardest for Patti and Noah, they say, is when Caden realizes he's different than other people. They can feel his heartbreak. They understand his desire to belong, and they do everything in their power to make that happen. The couple firmly believes in inclusion and never making preconceived notions about what people are capable of or what can bring joy into life. Noah's goal, in particular, is to treat his son like a fully healthy teenager and offer him the structure and support he needs to help him succeed behaviorally and socially. To help him thrive, the couple opens him up to new experiences as often as possible, including taking him to concerts. To Caden, a concert is anytime music is playing and he can dance, whether that's in front of a stage or in front of a musician playing an instrument on the street. Patti recalls a particularly special moment when, for his birthday, she and Noah took Caden to an Andrea Bocelli concert. She looked over at his face and saw such profound peace and connection. Such hope.

Besides music, Caden also loves traveling—especially planes, trains, automobiles, and hotels. On one of their earlier trips to New York as a new family with Patti, Caden had toured the city wide-eyed, holding Patti's hand and learning about some of her more notable neighbors from the old neighborhood. Though he can't remember directions from thirty seconds prior, he has a unique and astounding ability to recall cars, people, and places from his earliest years. It's the kind of remarkable recall that many with autism have, though Caden is not autistic. Once, out of the blue, while watching *60 Minutes* with Patti, Caden said, "Leslie Stahl, Patti's neighbor." It was a tiny fact he'd learned six years ago—at age nine—on that early trip to New York.

These memories are all reminders that because Caden's brain short-circuits a lot, the things that help him slow down are also some of the things the rest of us can take for granted in everyday life: friends, animals, music, hugs, interesting facts. He doesn't see color, age, or disability. He has all the ingredients of a happy and hopeful life, and he is willing to share them.

His friends and family don't view him by his diagnosed symptoms or as intellectually disabled. He is just Caden who continually surprises and delights everyone he touches. When the family does receive reminders of his limitations, it can be especially hard to accept and integrate emotionally.

That said, Patti and Noah don't want to gloss over the challenging parts of being parents of a child with a disability. It is emotionally and physically difficult, and they know that to say anything else would be dishonest. The hardest part, they say, is the unknown—and there's so much unknown with Caden. How do they know all that he is capable of? How do they help him reach his potential?

One thing they do know is that Caden is so incredibly loved. His passion for people and friendship is inspiring. When it comes to the general ed students he interacts with at school, his parents wonder whether he is getting more out of that time, or if it's the other way around.

What Patti and Noah want people to understand—and what they hope you'll take away from their story—is that it's not always about therapy in these situations; it's about inclusion. People who are differently-abled need different things, but they also *give* different things. It would be a huge mistake to limit them in life.

In closing, both families say that life with Caden is rewarding, but above the traditional sense. It's deeper. He creates relationships with people and changes everyone he comes into contact with, even if he's being defiant or difficult in the moment. Noah says Caden will wear you down while winning you over; he'll act out when he's with you, but as soon as he leaves, there's an emptiness. Every day, he reminds the family to let go, forgive, and accept.

BEAU'S STORY

BEAU, WHO TURNED TWO ON NEW YEAR'S EVE, started to pull up to stand last Christmas—a gift you can't wrap. He loves human interaction and animals. To say hello, he's fond of grabbing people's faces and staring into their eyes, smiling sweetly. It's that sweetness, in fact, that his mom Kim calls his hallmark.

"Beau is definitely the sweet one in the family," she laughs. "My daughter [Beau's older sister, Sutton] is the wild one, so they balance each other out nicely."

Beau is also hearing-aided and nonverbal, and it's unclear so far as to his level of understanding. There are many unknowns, in fact, because Beau has an extremely rare genetic condition called 16q11.2-12.2 microdeletion. There are only a handful of other children in the world who have this condition—one that causes kidney disease, hearing loss, low muscle tone, developmental delays, sensory processing issues, and perhaps autism.

When Kim and her husband Keith finally received Beau's diagnosis—specifically the genetic condition alongside nephronophthisis (kidney disease that would require a transplant later in life), a heart murmur, and a thin corpus callosum (the bridge between the two halves of the brain) that would cause developmental delays—they were...relieved.

That's because the doctors initially suspected Beau had Rett Syndrome, which they'd relayed was normally fatal in boys. Kim and Keith spent many long days and nights over the course of the week they lived with that possible diagnosis mourning the probable loss of their child.

"We wondered how we would go home to an empty nursery and tell our daughter her brother isn't coming home,"' Kim recalls. "When they told us he didn't have Rett's, we laughed right there in the room. The doctors asked if we were okay, and we said we were just so relieved and thankful. It was the best-case scenario for us. I had been worried I wouldn't be able to deal with losing Beau and be that strong person for our family, but since we got to keep him, I knew we could deal with whatever life would throw at us."

Life had, indeed, thrown a lot at them in a relatively short time. After a healthy pregnancy and normal genetic testing and ultrasounds, Kim and Keith didn't expect anything other than a smooth-as-possible hospital birth. The delivery itself was just that: normal. But as soon as Beau was delivered, Kim noticed he was floppy and would squirm out of her arms when she tried to place him on her chest. He also had a few ear tags and wasn't crying much. She wasn't worried, though, because she'd heard the medical team call out her son's APGAR scores—not perfect, but not terrible, either.

Kim's OB-GYN, whom she trusted and was very comfortable with, lingered in the delivery room a bit longer than usual, watching Kim try to get Beau to latch.

"I remember him [the doctor] saying 'hmm, that's interesting,'" she recalls. "And he was paying extra attention to what I was doing, watching me interact with Beau. He'd also spent a little time with him when he measured and weighed him. At that point, I still didn't think anything of it."

The doctor and nurses left the room and came back about ten minutes later. Kim asked if the family would be able to leave that day, something they'd discussed prior and was potentially doable. Her doctor replied that normally, yes, he'd let them go home—but not this time, as there was something wrong with Beau.

"He just said the transport NICU team from a hospital

in Northern Alberta were on their way, and that there were some things they needed to check out," Kim recalls. "When I asked what, he said Beau's ear tags, dislocated left hip, low muscle tone, and features consistent with congenital abnormalities—a flat nasal bridge, wide set eyes, lower set ears, cramped and overlapped toes—all together pointed to something they weren't equipped to deal with."

Keith went with Beau to the hospital in Alberta while she stayed behind to recover. When they tried to feed Beau in the hospital post-transfer, he immediately aspirated, resulting in a NG tube placement. Kim joined her family as soon as she was released, and together she and Keith watched helplessly for weeks as Beau suffered apnea episode after apnea episode, with no clear answers.

Once the cause was pinpointed, the family was able to pack up and move from the NICU to a regular floor.

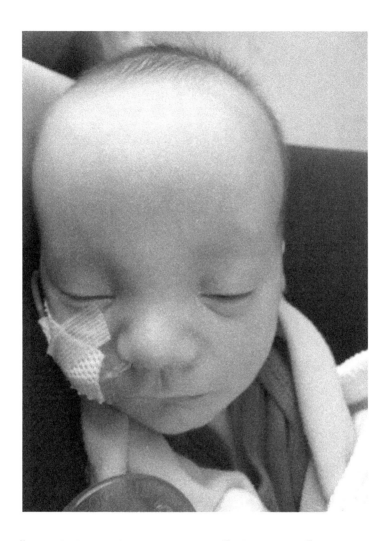

"We cried a lot of happy tears then," Kim recalls. "We could sleep in there with him, bond. And his sister could come more, too. It was better for all of us."

After Beau was able to come home, Kim says she continued the grieving process she'd felt when they first took him to the NICU, the air heavy with unknowns.

"I was quiet about Beau, not sharing much with family and friends, because I didn't want anyone to look at him and judge him. I wanted them to see Beau for Beau, nothing else."

After three or four months, she started sharing more on social media—slowly. First, she talked about her son's severe hearing loss as a consequence of his genetic condition. She opened up more and more, usually over Instagram, to introduce her son to the world.

"It was such a hard time," she recalls. "Then, I had a twenty-month-old daughter, my husband was away working long hours in the oil fields, and I had a lot of grief. I still grieve my child's life, to a degree. I see my friends' kids born around the same time as Beau, and they're joining dance or soccer or walking. That's not my journey with Beau, and I would be lying if I said it didn't hurt. That said, part of advocating for Beau is knowing that our adventure with him will be different, but just as beautiful. Every tiny thing with Beau is something to celebrate and appreciate."

Today, Beau has spent quite a bit of time in and out of hospitals or therapies. He's had one hip surgery and spent three months in a full body cast. He has a g-tube for fluids, though he does take 50-75 percent of his daily calories orally—some progress the family is happy to celebrate.

Other developments worth celebrating include Beau's results from Anat Baniel Method (ABM) therapy, a neuroplasticity-based therapy that meets children where they are. Thanks to gracious donations from their community through a GoFundMe campaign, Kim and Keith were able to take Beau to the ABM Center in California when he was one. There, the team worked with him for five days.

"Before we left, Beau was 100 percent tube dependent, not crawling or sitting. He was rolling, but only one way," Kim says. "But shortly after we got home, he started sitting up on his own. He ate a whole pouch of baby food, which was astonishing. Sometimes he's kind of off in Beau-land, but I started to see some things click for him."

Besides ABM for Beau, the couple has also been focusing on intense physiotherapy, occupational therapy, speech—all of it. They're currently waiting to see if their son will receive an autism or cerebral palsy diagnosis as well, which will help them determine how to move forward therapeutically.

At home, Beau is doted on by his sister, Sutton.

"Sometimes, she will ask why her brother doesn't walk or talk or something," Kim says. "And we tell her he is learning things in his own way and on his own time, and that's okay because that's who he is. She'll bring him toys and is so kind to him. She will be a great advocate for her brother one day. I'm excited that I get to see their special dynamic and watch how they grow together."

He is, of course, also doted on by his parents.

"For my husband, taking care of Beau came naturally. He's very type A, and what should get done gets done," Kim says. "I'm not so type A, but it also has come naturally to me, to a degree. Prior to Beau, I worked as a disability aide and social worker in my community. It was easy for me to step into that role. Plus, as a mama bear, it's not even a question. When I was pregnant, I was worried about having kids so close together. But once he was here, just looking at him, I thought 'your soul is so perfect for us.' He's always the one nuzzling into you and cuddling."

Even mama bears, though, need support.

Kim has reached out to the few other parents of children with Beau's condition—one in the UK and two in the US—and they've found community. Though no two journeys are the same, she knows what these families share can provide a glimpse into what to expect. That, and the hard-won understanding of fellow parents of children who are differently-abled.

As a mother in this community, Kim says it's unhelpful

and even hurtful when those with neurotypical children say, "I couldn't do it," or "I'm so sorry." Instead, it means so much when these parents can simply acknowledge that they don't understand but listen anyway. That—and treat Beau and family normally and with compassion.

"I read something shortly after my son was born that said special needs parenting isn't a sprint—it's a marathon," she says. "Two years in now, I see what they mean. You have to pace yourself."

Kim's advice to families facing a challenging diagnosis is to go heavy on the grace. If you don't get everything done in one day—all the cleaning, all the treatments—it's okay. Sometimes, Kim says, it's good to just enjoy your child and not get stuck in caregiver mode.

Being in caregiver mode is a big part of raising a child who is differently-abled, though, and Kim knows that all too well. Beau may need lifelong support. He will always have medical issues, and there are many unknowns around whether he may someday develop benign brain tumors, a potential complication of his genetic condition down the road.

"For some reason, I just know that all of this will be worth it," Kim says. "In fact, it already is. It's hard for someone who hasn't lived it to understand. This isn't the journey I would have chosen, but now that I'm on it, I feel like my whole life has led up to being Beau's mom. This is where we're all meant to be."

RYLAND'S STORY

DANA HARMON'S OLDEST SON, COLE, WAS BORN unexpectedly at thirty-five weeks. She and her husband felt lucky that, despite his premature entrance into the world, Cole was healthy. During her second pregnancy with son, Ryland, Dana's primary worry was whether Ryland would arrive ahead of schedule, too.

He didn't.

"With Cole, we got a little taste of how birth can be very unexpected," she recalls. "And with Ryland, we got a big taste of how unexpected issues can pop up down the line."

Dana and Ryland left the hospital two days after his smooth, full-term birth. It was the middle of summer, and Dana and her husband Jeff settled into taking care of not one, but two young children. The only visitors they had over that first week were grandparents, preferring family time at home over going out in public.

The morning of his seventh day on Earth, Ryland—who before had breastfed without any major issue—began having feeding challenges. Dana breastfed Cole, so she had an inkling something was off.

"That morning, Ryland wasn't having full feeds, but he'd still latch," she remembers. "As the day progressed, he wouldn't even latch anymore. I tried pumping, but he wouldn't take the bottle."

On top of the feeding issues, Ryland could barely stay awake; he was sleeping far more than usual and was difficult to rouse. He was already a sleepy eater, so she wondered if that was contributing to the issue. To test her theory, Dana used an old trick: take off her son's clothes and rub him, hoping the cold would force him awake enough to eat.

Then, something clicked when she felt his skin. He was warm—"but not bundled-up-baby warm, warm-warm."

Dana told Jeff that something wasn't right. The only thermometer they had in the house wouldn't work for a newborn, so they called their neighbors and best friends— one of whom happened to be a nurse—who rushed to their aid with a rectal thermometer. Ryland's temperature was 100.2, right under the fever guidelines for a newborn. Jeff thought everything was probably fine, but Dana insisted on reaching out to the pediatric on-call nurse.

"At that point, I was freaking out," Dana recalls. "Part of it was hormones, but another part was that I just knew my baby was sick. The nurse agreed with me and said the number on the thermometer didn't matter that much at the moment."

After the nurse affirmed Ryland needed to be seen,

Dana asked her friends to stay at her house, where Cole still slept upstairs in his crib. She and Jeff grabbed the diaper bag with what was already in it, threw on sandals to accompany their lounge clothes, and drove the fifteen minutes to Cincinnati Children's Hospital Main Campus. En route, Dana texted her mom to ask her to come care for Cole. She didn't call because she was holding out hope that it could still be nothing, and saying the words out loud could have broken that feeling.

When they got to the ER, the situation spiraled downward. After explaining the issue and briefly filling out paperwork, the nurses brought the family back ahead of others in line—an indication that this was serious. They moved Ryland to a triage room and then to a regular ER room, where they noticed his breath-holding spells. From there, he was moved to "trauma bay," an area where the full team could work on Ryland at once and where a rush was placed on all orders. After they completed the work-up in trauma bay—the taking of his urine, bloodwork, and cerebral and spinal fluid as well as an assessment of his respiratory state—Ryland was admitted to the NICU. There, he was put on oxygen, but that was just the start. Over the course of the next three days, the seven-day-old infant was intubated, placed on a continuous EEG, and suffered seizures. He was in a state of paralysis, unable to be held by his worried parents—who were taking turns going home to take care of and comfort Cole.

Then, on the last panel of tests the doctors were running before diagnosing Ryland with viral meningitis, they found the answer: human parechovirus-3, which resulted in secondary viral meningoencephalitis. It was the first-ever case of that particular virus in Cincinnati Children's Hospital.

"The team came by around midnight, and the doctor was very excited that we had an answer. But it also wasn't the greatest news in the world," Dana says. "Over the next two weeks, Ryland made it through the worst of it, they got his seizures under control, and we went through the days-long journey back to room air [i.e., coming off of oxygen] and nursing."

Before discharge, the neurologist met with the family to discuss an MRI of Ryland's brain—one that showed significant global white matter damage. The medical team said there was no way of knowing how the brain damage would manifest for Ryland—he could meet some milestones but have delays, he could have epilepsy, he could have cerebral palsy...nobody knew.

"They told us to take him home, take care of him, love him, and follow up," Dana says. "Jeff and I quickly knew that we would be okay with whatever Ryland's challenges would be—but the not knowing was the hardest part."

In February 2019, at seven months old, Ryland was diagnosed with cerebral palsy. Though an earlier-than-average diagnosis, his medical team was highly confident in their assessment—and the family was hopeful having a diagnosis would grant them access to more opportunities for therapies, such as those at the widely regarded NAPA Center.

"Of course we didn't come home from the NICU hoping for that diagnosis," Dana says. "But we knew we'd do whatever we needed to do for Ryland, no matter what."

Today, Ryland is almost two. His diagnosis is still cerebral palsy, unspecified. The family has done and continues to do everything they can for Ryland—no appointment, specialist, or therapy has been off limits. He's had outpatient physical therapy and visited the Perlman Center at

Cincinnati Children's for group therapy, including physical therapy, occupational therapy, and speech/feeding therapy. Perlman gave Ryland the chance to do one-on-one therapies as well as participate in these group therapies, many that involved singing and playing with other children. It is at Perlman, Dana recalls, that they "learned the most about how to integrate opportunities into daily life to maximize Ryland's experiences."

That daily life piece is important because, from the beginning, Dana and Jeff felt it was critical that the family lead as normal a life as possible. Dana, for example, went back to work when Ryland was four months old. Since then, Ryland has attended the Goddard School with his older brother.

"He's been healthy, so there's not a whole lot to lean on medically," Dana says. "It's all about therapy and development."

After the shelter-in-place orders were instituted during the COVID-19 crisis, childcare closed, and Jeff, unfortunately, got laid off. This felt like the perfect time to take action on a question the family had been wrestling with before the germs hit: Should they keep Ryland at Goddard or keep him home? As he transitioned from baby to toddler, his delays were becoming more apparent. Both Dana and Jeff had agreed that they needed to give Ryland the best chance at whatever independence he could gain later. That meant looking for more opportunities to work with him one-on-one and with more intentionality than childcare could provide. They made an important decision: Jeff does not plan to return to work post COVID-19 lockdown—a big step for the family and for Ryland.

"We are excited to see what the future holds," Dana says of this next adventure.

But the adventure they're on now hasn't been without exploration—far from it. Dana finds that having Cole so close in age to Ryland sometimes leads her to unintentionally compare milestones, but it also pushes the family to do more.

"I often think it's both good and bad that we have an older child who is neurotypical. There's the comparison piece—'Cole was doing this at Ryland's age'—and things like that, but it also helps with the normalcy," she says. "I can't look at a playground Cole wants to go to and say we can't because I'm not sure how Ryland will handle it. Having them both forces us to figure it out. And we do. We just figure it out."

Dana is quick to point out that the sense of normalcy she and her family cherish is *not* the same thing as ignoring the reality of Ryland's diagnosis.

"Ryland's disability isn't going to limit our opportunities or experiences as a family," she says. "It's not 'something to deal with.' It's *part* of our normal. How could it not be? Ryland has had the sweetest demeanor from day one. He likes picking on his big brother, and he has a great sense of humor already. We're just starting to see his personality develop, and he's perfect for us."

JADEN'S STORY

NICOLETTE RICHER HAS LONG BEEN A FEARLESS advocate for her children's health, using both her deep research of the power of nutrition and her maternal instinct, in equal doses.

Nicolette's oldest daughter, Jaden, was born with a lymphatic drainage issue, meaning she gets aggressively sick and doesn't heal from infections like other children naturally do.

When her baby was only ten days old, Nicolette and her husband rushed her to the doctor at 6:00 pm one evening. Nicolette recalls that she just knew something was off, but the attending physician didn't reciprocate her urgency at first. The doctor told the family to go home and return in a few days if the baby wasn't better.

As she stepped out of the office and heard the click of the door behind her, though, Nicolette knew she couldn't accept that. She turned around and started banging on the door of the now-locked facility until the doctor—who was, at that point, annoyed—let them back in.

"I don't care," Nicolette remembers saying. "I am not leaving until I get a 100 percent guarantee that my daughter is okay."

At Nicolette's insistence, the doctor undressed and reexamined the infant. That's when she found a golf ball-sized mass under the baby's breast. The doctor picked up the phone immediately and called the hospital to report the emergency situation.

"It was terrifying," Nicolette recalls. "And the way they treated me before that—with all the questions and them just expecting me to take their word—it made me feel like I was crazy. Clearly, I wasn't."

The severe infections happened again when her daughter was four and then nine. In both instances, Nicolette advocated for days to get the testing and treatment her daughter needed, often at the pushback of doctors. She has been told several times that had she not brought her daughter in or gotten her the treatments she did, her daughter would have died.

Nicolette had to flex her mom advocacy muscle in a different way a few years later when her daughter got a concussion while playing on an aerial yoga swing at her friend's house. Another tween got the incident on video, and when Nicolette saw her daughter's head smashing onto the floor, she knew what had happened. Even though her daughter was acting okay after the initial incident, she mentioned light bothered her, as well as some normal sounds (like a fork scraping the glass plate at dinner). Nicolette and her husband took their daughter to the doctor, where a concussion was confirmed.

The specialist they saw next—a sports medicine doctor specializing in concussions—said Nicolette's daughter passed all the physical tests (eye movement, etc.) and would need to stay out of school until she could read a few sentences without exacerbating her already-disruptive headache. However, that never happened.

Nicolette recalls finding it strange that there was no neurological scanning or data collection besides the physical testing, but she followed the doctor's recommendations—at first.

When Nicolette's daughter did try to go back to school, she'd last about thirty minutes before needing to be picked up because her headache was usually "a thirteen out of ten" on the pain scale. Mostly, she stayed home, and the family did whatever she needed—kept quiet, the lights low. It seemed to work in the short term, but it wasn't a long-term solution. Her daughter had always loved school and wanted to go back. Nicolette wasn't accepting the "wait and see" approach.

"I couldn't stand to see her in pain for one more day," she recalls.

So, she took her daughter into the ER and demanded answers. She was told they'd seen lots of concussions and that it could be up to a year before the symptoms completely went away.

Shocked by that answer and by the lack of resources she was finding in traditional medicine, Nicolette says, "the mama bear came out" in her.

"I said 'forget all that,'" she says. "I went back to all my neuroscience research. I thought of everything someone might do if they had an autistic child. Then, I wondered what would happen if I just went crazy and did it all—MCT [medium-chain triglycerides] oil, flax oil, lions mane, plant-based, high carb foods—every supplement, every food, every physical therapy I know that supports the brain."

The family already followed a plant-based diet, so they had the food on hand for Nicolette to make her daughter brain-boosting meals. After leaving the ER, she made same-day appointments—for physio, acupuncture, and optometry (to buy rose-colored glasses and tape off the periphery).

She also made an appointment at a magnesium float tank that focuses on sensory deprivation, as the most effective way to transport magnesium is transdermally. Nicolette knew that people who have brain injuries or learning disabilities often take the supplement orally and transdermally (through the skin). She likens the float tank experience as akin to "floating in the Dead Sea."

Four and a half hours later—before lunch—they were home, all those appointments under their belts. Then, Nicolette started compression therapy.

"People who are autistic or have neurological sensitivity often find their peripheral and central nervous systems are out of alignment or overloaded. In these patients, some doctors use compression vests to calm the nervous system and stimulate the release of feel good hormones like serotonin and oxytocin. I wondered what would happen if I compressed every inch of my daughter's body, depriving her of all input so that her nervous system had time to be calm. Then, she could benefit from hyper-communication from the brain, as there would be nothing for her body to fight against. I wanted to stimulate that regenerative healing."

Nicolette gathered every pillow in the house, even bean bag pillows, and covered her daughter, leaving only her nostrils and mouth exposed. She slept like that for 2.5 hours—the longest she'd slept since her concussion. When she woke up, she reported her pain at a one—the first time in an entire month it had been even below a six.

Nicolette was pleased but expected the pain to creep back up, as it usually did. She fed her another brain-healthy meal. Then, she took her daughter to the chiropractor and asked her to align the child completely.

"When your body is perfectly aligned, you don't have compression in your spinal cord. That way, the neurological transmission can get to all parts of the body and stimulate healing," she explains.

Her pain level after that visit? Zero.

"That night at dinner, we didn't have to worry about our forks scraping or keeping the curtains closed," Nicolette says. "She went to school the next day and didn't miss another day until she got another concussion two years later from snowboarding—and I treated it the same way."

This method is one Nicolette suggests to anyone with a chronic illness, as it's rooted in triggering the body's ability to heal itself. She applied the same treatment to a client who had been suffering with symptoms from a concussion sustained way back in 1996. After two weeks, her symptoms were gone, too.

"Compression is one of the most beneficial things you can do for your body because it stimulates the lymphatic system. If everybody were to do compression therapy for half an hour to an hour a day; eat a healthy, plant-based diet; and restore nutrient deficiencies, we'd see a decrease in every chronic disease," she says.

BRAYDEN'S STORY

JENNIFER HOGAN'S FIRST PREGNANCY WAS GOING smoothly, for the most part. At twenty years old, she was healthy and excited to meet her son. Then, in the last couple of months, she started having high blood pressure and began to gain weight very quickly. Because preeclampsia ran in her family, the doctor put Jennifer on bed rest. A week-and-a-half before her son, Brayden, was due, she laid down for a whole hour and didn't feel one movement. Because this was her first pregnancy, she'd been extra valiant to do everything the doctor said; taking kick counts religiously, etc. The non-movement, then, felt extra alarming. She called her doctor, who told her to lie on her side. When that didn't work, she went to the hospital.

What happened next was traumatic. Unbeknownst to Jennifer or her doctors, her placenta had started to detach when she first got to the hospital. No ultrasound was ever conducted. Her doctor indicated the baby was in distress and would need to be delivered that night, so he said he'd come back after dinner. In the meantime, Jennifer was moved into a delivery room, and the nurse put her on a Pitocin drip without verifying with the doctor. That sent her body into shock, and the hospital called her doctor to return. Jennifer had lost control over her body. She was shaking and could still hear and see, but she couldn't talk.

The doctor arrived fifteen minutes later, and they rushed Jennifer into the emergency room for a C-section. The anesthesiologist wasn't at the hospital, so they had to page him. But before he arrived, they had to put Jennifer completely to sleep, and she recalls them telling her they'd likely lost her son. She woke up not knowing if Bray was alive. Later, they'd find out that because of the loss of oxygen to his brain, he had been dead for over fifteen minutes.

Finally, the doctor told Jennifer that Bray was alive—but likely would not live more than two days. He was transferred to another hospital, but Jennifer was not permitted to accompany him because she was still recovering from her C-section. She advocated for herself and convinced the staff to release her in two days, however, so she could be with Brayden.

He defied the doctors' prognosis, living longer than two days. Today, Brayden (or "Bray" or "Bubba," as they call him), is fourteen. (Jennifer later won a lawsuit against the hospital where her son was born.)

Before he came home, Brayden spent fifteen days in the NICU and was diagnosed with a Traumatic Brain Injury that affected primarily the left side of his brain.

"He was the biggest baby in there, and nobody knew what to expect," Jennifer recalls. "Over the next six months, he continued to not meet the 'normal' baby milestones. He would always have clenched fists, screaming most of the time. The only time he didn't scream was when I was holding him—so I did, all the time."

Brayden was making some sounds at six months old, but not many. He also had major difficulty drinking from a bottle. Jennifer recalls it could take him up to two hours to swallow three ounces of formula, as his sucking and swallowing were very labored. As a result, he was not gaining weight and would go on to have a g-tube placed. The doctors told Jennifer they didn't like to diagnose children at that age, but Jennifer was eager to pinpoint what she could do to assist her son.

Around the same time as the surgery, Brayden was diagnosed with Spastic Quadriplegia Cerebral Palsy (CP), affecting all his limbs. Later, when Brayden was two-and-a-half, Jennifer learned her son had Cystic Fibrosis, as well.

"For all special needs parents, I think there's a point where someone tells you 'it will get better,' and you don't believe it. The first year-and-a-half with Brayden, it was so hard. It's still so hard today, and that's the truth. But it does get better. I never thought I'd learn to feed my kid through a g-tube, for example, but you learn together."

Jennifer tried several therapies when Brayden was young, such as Botox injections to help spasticity in his legs, abductor surgery, and braces. It was when Jennifer took Brayden to do Anat Baniel Method (ABM) Therapy when he was four-and-a-half, though, that she really saw changes. During his time in therapy, his trunk strengthened, he learned to roll over, his hands loosened up, and more. A year later, when Jennifer won the lawsuit against the hospital and was in a better spot financially, she was able to bring Brayden to ABM more frequently. For two years, they went for one week out of each month, and Brayden was thriving.

"ABM was amazing for us," Jennifer recalls. "Brayden started to make more sounds, and he could eat baby food. At his best, he could hold his head up, he could sit Indian style, and it was easy for him to reach for things. At school, he was using his head to toggle switches on the sides of his wheelchair, so he could use his head to push buttons and play games.

When he was eleven, though, he had an accident while

at his father's house (from whom Jennifer was then separated). He'd fallen out of bed, and his brain started to swell because his skull was fractured.

"The surgeon told me I should think about just letting him go," Jennifer recalls. "But Bray has always been super strong and a fighter. They did the surgery and airlifted him to Portland Children's Hospital, where he spent over a week in a coma. When he woke up, we found out he'd also suffered a few little strokes. They thought maybe he'd be blind, but he wasn't."

Today, Bray is "back to square one" from where he was progress-wise. Jennifer holds him because he no longer has head or trunk control. She has a caregiver who helps Brayden when he's at her house and also when he's at his dad's. The caregiver helps with breathing treatments, giving multiple medications, changing him, dropping him off at school, etc. Jennifer now has two other children, too, so her plate is more than full at home.

"It's been frustrating and heartbreaking, seeing how he's gone backward," she says. "Since his most recent surgery last spring, he has a CPAP he needs to wear at night. Some nights he will wear it, and others he screams for it to come off."

Today, Bray can communicate using eye movements, but Jennifer says it's harder overall now—as are most things.

Treatment-wise, Jennifer is trying to decide how to best care for Brayden. Recently, she has been rubbing CBD (Cannabidiol) cream on his muscles, which seems to help them relax.

"After the accident, I went into a depression," Jennifer says. "That's when I really needed someone. Sometimes it's hard to hold onto positivity. If you're a parent of a kid like Bray, it's likely that most of your friends who have typical children can't relate to what you're going through. They just can't. That's why it's so important that you have people in your life who really get it. That's what I learned, especially during that time."

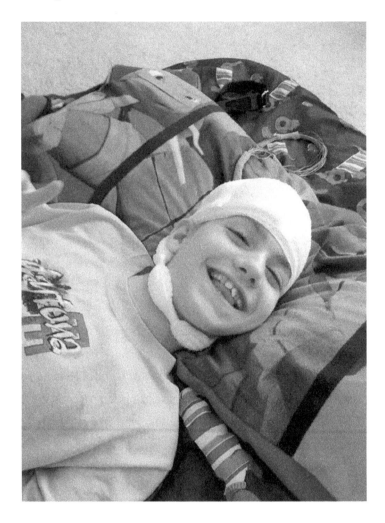

Advocating for her son has been a huge part of Jennifer's life, as well. She encourages parents to follow their gut feelings and ask questions, even if it feels uncomfortable at first.

When describing her son, Jennifer wants the world to know Bray has his challenges, but they do not define him.

"It's a miracle that he's here with us. He has a super happy personality. He reminds and teaches you about real joy," she says. "Bray is a fighter and has taught me so much about life and the world through this journey. He truly touches everyone he meets."

DIERKS' STORY

JESSICA UNDERWOOD WAS THIRTY-FIVE WEEKS AND five days pregnant with her son, Dierks. The family was at her son Simon's fifth birthday party. As it was her sixth pregnancy, Jessica was experiencing Braxton Hicks contractions that felt real. Her blood pressure was also high. She called the doctor, who said she should come in and get checked out.

All of her other babies were born a couple days late, so Jessica wasn't worried about Dierks arriving early. That said, she had seen some discrepancies between this pregnancy and her others. For example, she'd become very swollen. In retrospect, Jessica recalls that Dierks kicked a ton around twenty to twenty-eight weeks, and she can almost pinpoint the weekend where she started to swell and not feel the baby as much. None of this registered that day, though.

In the hospital, on August 13, as Jessica was hooked up to the monitors, the doctors could see that the baby's heart rate was steady. When she contracted, though, the heart rate decelerated (they didn't know at the time whether it was a boy or girl). The baby was also breech. The couple had planned on doing external cephalic version (EVC) therapy the following week to manually flip the baby, but the doctor said there was no time.

Jessica recalls crying because she had to have a C-section. She still wasn't thinking there could be something wrong with her baby, with everything going on. After Dierks was born at 7:11 pm—again, on Simon's birthday— the nurse brought her son over to Jessica. Dierks was bruised, and the nursing staff asked if any of her other children had the same issue at birth.

They didn't.

The team took Dierks to the NICU to investigate the bruising, where initial bloodwork revealed that his platelets were low. The low platelets led to a CAT scan. At this time, Jessica was still in her hospital room, waiting for Dierks to come back. Instead, the doctor knocked on the door and told her that the CAT scan showed that her newborn son had a very serious brain bleed and would need to be transferred to a specialty hospital, Children's Mercy, where he would have access to specialists.

Thank God, Jessica's doctor let her accompany Dierks to the hospital—something many physicians may not have advised, considering she'd just given birth.

When the family arrived at Children's Mercy, it was, as Jessica describes, "a day of bad news that felt full of goodbyes." She recalls the doctors checking the chart over and over while glancing at the kicking, healthy-appearing baby—it didn't match up. But the test results were grim. An MRI—which took a long time (not a good sign)—showed the entire right side of his brain had shifted over to make room for the blood. It was a Grade 4 Bleed with blood in multiple parts of the brain, something the doctors remarked they'd never seen.

The next day and the day after, as Dierks fought on, the team started talking to Jessica and her husband Chris about surgery. It was something Jessica was looking forward to—anything to get the blood out. The neurosurgeon who was to perform the surgery had a reputation for being gruff. Jessica recalls googling him before the procedure and, in meeting him, making the same assessment. She felt lost and afraid, telling the neurosurgeon, "I understand you do this every day, but this is the only time I've done this. You're cutting into my baby's brain." He was very responsive to that and softened a little—something Jessica and her husband appreciated.

On August 29, the neurosurgeon and his team did a washout, or a dime-size incision to remove the blood. Then, they did an MRI every few days to watch for hydrocephalus and ensure the bleeding had stopped.

The surgeon remarked that the blood in Dierks's brain had been there for months, indicating the bleed happened sometime in utero. Jessica recalls thinking that had they done the EVC therapy as they'd planned, Dierks likely wouldn't have survived. It's just one of many miracles she credits to God—including the fact that her doctor let her go with Dierks to the hospital, as that was one of the hardest days for her baby boy.

All told, Dierks spent three months in the neonatal intensive care unit (NICU). It was little thing after little thing that would prevent him from going home—blood in the stool, low blood sugar, continuous feeds because he never learned to drink from a bottle. Every day, Jessica and her husband would go to the chapel and quickly say the rosary. They credit a higher power for giving them grace during those trying days.

His release day was a joyous one. Although he was technically three months old, Jessica says that day felt a little like his birthday. For a while after, Children's Mercy Home Care visited the family every couple of days. Then, those visits waned after the family opted-in to weekly occupational therapy with First Steps, a publicly funded program in Missouri that started in January 2019. Jessica says this has been helpful because even though Dierks is her sixth baby, there have been so many lessons she's taken away from these OT sessions that have reminded her what she can be looking for or working on to help Dierks thrive.

Not only lessons—but so much to be thankful for, too. In particular, Jessica recalls how grateful she felt when the therapist looked at her son, surprised, and remarked how the boy in front of him didn't match the boy reflected in the chart. Not every family's journey includes a moment like that—a fact of which she is well aware—and she and her husband feel beyond blessed.

Today, over a year later, Dierks is healthy, happy, and home. He'd long had a g-tube (unrelated to his brain bleed) but was able to have it removed shortly after his first birthday because the doctors were satisfied with his eating and his growth. This was a huge milestone: the family no longer had to worry about Dierks pulling his tube out and packing extra supplies for every outing. But most of all, it was another affirmation that Dierks was a healthy baby boy who loves to eat.

There have been other milestones. In fact, as of this writing, Dierks is hitting them all. And, though Jessica knows his journey may not be over, she's quick to note the marked difference between where her son was when he was born and where he is today.

"It's night and day—a true miracle."

There have been more miracles. Before Dierks, Jessica recalls that she had no experience with brain injury whatsoever. When she first heard "brain bleed," she wasn't ready for hope. She was terrified and heartbroken. She was still digesting the fact that her baby wasn't "perfect," and her mind went immediately to the worst-case scenario. She didn't realize all the different levels of brain injury or understand the options.

It wasn't until days later she remembered something someone had told her when she was deep in that fog. It was a story of another baby who had a brain bleed and recovered. In the moment of deep hurt, it got lost, but she came back to it and let it warm her when she was ready.

Jessica says she is grateful for Dierks and the many miracles in her life. She is careful to say she is not bragging about how well Dierks is doing—rather, in sharing his story—she hopes to be like the story in the fog for another family.

Today, Jessica says she's a firm believer that most brain injuries can be helped and supported with therapy. She believes the brain is an amazing thing, especially in a newborn—it's changing, creating pathways, growing. It's full of hope. A diagnosis is not an ending point, it's a starting point for growth.

GRAYDEN'S STORY

WHEN KELLY AND HER HUSBAND AUSTIN WENT FOR their twenty-week ultrasound, they learned that their son (to be named Grayden) had a severe form of spina bifida, specifically myelomeningocele, the most severe form. This means that early on in the pregnancy, Grayden's spine did not fuse as it should have. As a result, the spinal cord was outside the spinal column, protruding from his back.

As of this writing, almost a decade later, this family has grown in many ways. Grayden is now almost ten, and his brother Kinsen is five. Their older brother—who was only fifteen months old when Grayden's journey began—is now closing in on his teenage years.

"We were so scared of what this diagnosis would mean for our family and for Grayden's life. We experienced a lot of grief during those first months," Kelly says. "But today, we're focused on growth, health, and the pride we feel for all of the amazing things that Grayden is doing and learning."

Looking back, though, Kelly still remembers all of the details of the days and months after the spina bifida diagnosis was confirmed. Austin and Kelly had been referred to a maternal fetal specialist, a neurosurgeon, and other consulting doctors. The couple and their families acted on an individual level as well, researching and learning more about spina bifida and what treatment options were available. As Austin is an information seeker, he'd scoured a textbook from college that had details about the diagnosis. Kelly's research was more relational. She'd sought out stories rooted in other family's experiences with having a child with spina bifida.

Through their research, Kelly and Austin came across the Management of Myelomeningocele Study (MOMS), a federally funded clinical trial being conducted at the Children's Hospital of Philadelphia. This study was aimed at reducing the impact of spina bifida through fetal surgery. After a long process, Kelly decided to opt-in to the trial and was chosen in a randomized fashion to be a participant in the study.

When Grayden was twenty-five weeks gestation, he and Kelly underwent surgery to repair his spine and back in utero. Following fetal surgery, Kelly, her older son Zander, and rotating family members remained in Philadelphia until his birth. Nine weeks later, Grayden arrived. He was still six weeks premature and needed to spend almost a month at the hospital in the Neonatal Intensive Care Unit (NICU) to support his underdeveloped lungs.

This was a challenging time for the family as Kelly was far away from her home and support systems in Michigan. She was also missing Zander, who had returned home with family after Grayden's birth. But they juggled things as best they could, continuing the advocacy work they had started when their second son hadn't even yet entered the world. Kelly attributes some of her advocacy as having her background in occupational therapy for children ages birth to three.

When Grayden was about five months old, Kelly was introduced to a local Anat Baniel Method (ABM) practitioner. Attracted to ABM's strengths-based intervention methods, Kelly attended a two-day workshop with Anat Baniel, the mother of ABM Therapy. After attending the workshop, she began taking Grayden to work with the local ABM practitioner regularly—two days a week until he was four. Kelly also decided to sign up for the ABM practitioner training, where she then traveled to the ABM Center on the West Coast multiple times over the next three years, sometimes bringing Grayden along to receive lessons.

"What I loved most about Anat's work was that the focus was not on 'fixing' what was wrong with Grayden, but rather connecting with him and optimizing his strengths," she recalls. "I realized after hearing Anat speak that I never wanted Grayden to see himself as something that was 'broken,' but rather as a whole person who was valued just as he is."

As Grayden participated in ABM, Kelly recalls noticing

how fluidly he was able to move his body. They allowed him to follow his own timeline. By doing that, when he reached a developmental milestone, he did so with ease.

"When he was six, we slowed down with ABM," Kelly says. "He is doing so well now. I still like to go occasionally to keep his movements fluid and optimize how well he moves his body. We also have a deep connection with his ABM practitioner."

It wasn't just the physical rewards of ABM that drew Kelly to the therapy.

"I know so much of Anat's work focuses on the positives," she says. "We always looked at what Grayden had and not what he didn't have. That approach changed the direction I went with Grayden and the direction I take in my work. Somewhere along the way, I heard a quote that really stuck with me 'You can either see what you believe, or you can believe what you see.' Early on, doctors and other professionals had a very distinct view of what they believed Grayden would not do, and we looked more at the possibility of what he could."

Today, Grayden is thriving. He is determined, smart, silly, and kind. He loves playing with his brothers, eating sushi, watching YouTube videos, hanging out with friends, and being outdoors. He has also recently joined a local wheelchair basketball team, where he has continued to grow and form new connections.

In that determined and kind fashion, Grayden was gracious enough to share, in his own words, how his life is today. "Living with spina bifida doesn't feel that different. I can still do all of the things that I want to do!" he says. "It's fun to share my story."

Kelly is not sure if she should attribute Grayden's success to the early surgery, ABM, or a combination of the two—but what matters is that Grayden is healthy and happy.

"We have always advocated for Grayden and we always will," Kelly says, "but we want him to learn to advocate for himself, too. This is something that we are all continuing to learn as we go. We hold basically the same expectations for all of our kids. We ask that they give their best in all that they do."

"I think in the beginning I was so focused on what spina bifida was going to take away from our lives, that I wasn't able to realize all that this experience would teach us and all the ways that we would find new joy," she says. "I have met some incredible people along this journey, some of whom are now my very best friends. I can talk to them anytime. They get the hard stuff. They also get the joy in celebrating each thing we were told our kids may never do."

Kelly says parenting Grayden is just like parenting her other kids, Zander and Kinsen. There's just more thinking involved with some parts.

In fact, a lot of that thinking—particularly the *overthinking*—is what Kelly advises families to avoid when possible as they manage the emotions of a new diagnosis.

"Take it one step at a time," she suggests. "With Grayden, I initially worried way ahead. I worried what his life would be down the line. I thought about the what-ifs from his childhood to adulthood. Part of this is natural, and I get it. But Grayden has taught me that you cannot always plan for the future. He has taught me to live more in the present and to find joy in those moments rather than consuming my thoughts with the worries of tomorrow. No matter what, Grayden is still my child, worth celebrating every step of the way."

ACKNOWLEDGMENTS

THIS PROJECT WOULD NOT HAVE COME TOGETHER so beautifully—or, in some cases, at all—without the unyielding support and generosity of the following people:

My family. I know what it means to be a good person in this world because of all of you. Your no-strings-attached pride and faith in me has lifted me up in moments of which I'm quite sure you have no idea. Through it all, those pieces have never faltered. I love you. Thank you.

Scribe Media. This is no regular work perk. The perk part is the stone tossed into water, for which the reach of the ripples—and there are many—would not be possible. My gratitude for this gift is immeasurable because it allows me to reach so many *more* families who need hope and understanding. It already has. Thank you, Tribe.

The Brain Possible. Allison Murray and Mary Hawkins, your support on and enthusiasm for the Stories of Hope series, long before it blossomed into this book, means the world to me. I could have never made the connections I did, shared the stories with our audience, or collected all the behind-the-scenes requisite paperwork for this project without your social media prowess, organization, and offers of support without expiration dates. Thank you, friends.

M. The earnest and thoughtful feedback you provided at all levels of this project, from conception to now, elevated both the quality of this book and my confidence in bringing it to life. You loaned me your time and energy when both were in short supply, and I will not forget that. If I'm being honest, this book has always been a little bit for you. Thank you for seeing me.

Emily and Matt Abbott. Working on *Who Is Carter* all those years ago—and volunteering for each project that has come after it—has changed me. This work has taught me to listen harder and love bigger and appreciate deeper—and I'm not just talking about in what I do for the foundation. It started spilling over from day one and has not stopped. You are family to me. Thank you for letting me be a part of all the beauty Carter inspired.

ABOUT THE AUTHOR

JESSICA BURDG is a writer with a passion for personal narratives, creative nonfiction, and poetry. A journalist by trade, she uses her desire to learn about people and bring their stories into the world as a ghostwriter and Manuscript Creative at Scribe Media. Jessica has made a career helping authors turn their ideas into books; this is *her* first.

Jessica's essays and articles have been featured in multiple magazines and anthologies. Her essay on mental health was a finalist for the 2019 Conger J. Beasley Jr. Award for Nonfiction. After decades of only being lovingly displayed behind a refrigerator magnet in her late grandfather's kitchen, her poetry is now found at *Entropy Magazine*—and she knows he would be proud.

Jessica is a mother, experience-enthusiast, and music lover. She enjoys traveling, running, and underlining meaningful finds in her growing collection of hard copy books and newspapers. She lives in the Midwest with her young daughters, who mean everything.

Jessica cares about social and economic equality, children's literacy, women's rights—and, obviously, the differently-abled community. She is active in the non-profit space and is the founder of Project Penpal (www.projectpenpal.org), a foundation that fosters connection among lonely seniors in assisted living facilities with volunteer penpals around the country. She is the editorial chair of Who Is Carter and The Brain Possible, two organizations that work tirelessly to support the differently-abled community and those with pediatric brain injuries. Jessica also volunteers with Lead to Read, a project that pairs adult mentors/readers with elementary-aged children in under-resourced school districts in her area.

As are all human beings, Jessica is a work in progress. She also always has several works in progress; you can see what they are at www.JessicaBurdg.com.